London's Industrial Heritage

7153 4163 4

To B.W.

11/75
£3.95

Printed in Great Britain by
W. J. Holman Limited Dawlish
for David and Charles (Publishers) Ltd
South Devon House   Railway Station
Newton Abbot   Devon

London's Industrial Heritage

AUBREY WILSON

Photographs by JOSEPH McKEOWN

Research Assistant PENELOPE VOUSDEN

DAVID & CHARLES

NEWTON ABBOT · DEVON

CONTENTS

Introduction   *page* 6

Hydraulic Devil at St Katharine Docks   14

A Tide Mill at Bow   16

A Bramah Press at Chessington   18

Deptford East Power Station   20

The First Thames Tunnel   24

Textile Printing at Merton   28

Piano Factory in St Pancras   30

A Capital Patent Crane in the City   32

Abbey Mills Pumping Station   34

Gasholder at Fulham   38

Veneer Lathe in Mile End   40

Control Tower at Croydon Airport   42

Sewer Gas Lamp off the Strand   44

Relics from the Pre-history of Railways   46

An Old Hand-printing Press at Finsbury Park   48

An Umbrella Shop in Holborn   50

Pottery Kiln in Kensington   52

A Nineteenth-century Planing Machine in Eltham   54

A Candle Factory in Battersea   56

Coal Duty Posts   58

Water-Meter Testing Tower at Islington   60

Container Hoist in Clerkenwell   64

A Cold Rolling Machine at Bromley-by-Bow   66

The 'Round House' at Chalk Farm   68

Food-drying Kilns in Lambeth   70

Hermitage Inner Cutting Swing Bridge, London Docks   72

Margarine Factory in Southall   74

An Ether Plant at Ilford   78

Tower Bridge   80

Smithfield Market   82

Tower Bridge: a triumphant watergate to London

Spitalfields Silk Weavers' Houses 84

Fairground Music Punch in Clerkenwell 88

The Mint Stables at Paddington 90

Launching Site of the *Great Eastern*, Isle of Dogs 92

Brewery in Chiswell Street 96

Sealing-wax Factory in Bermondsey 98

Plate Edge-Planer, Isle of Dogs 100

Wooden Winch in St Paul's Cathedral 102

The Whitechapel Bell Foundry 104

Pumping Station at Kew Bridge 106

Snuff Mills at Morden 108

East India Company Warehouses, Bishopsgate 110

Clock Gearwheel-cutting Machine in Clerkenwell 112

The Regents Park Diorama 114

Remains of the Croydon Atmospheric Railway 116

Linoleum Presses at Staines 120

The Kingsway Tram Tunnel 122

The Brixton Windmill 126

The Wharncliffe Viaduct 128

Ram Brewery Beam Engines, Wandsworth 130

The Camden Town Catacombs 132

Offices in Fulham Road 134

An Overhead Crane at New Cross 136

The Copper Mill in Walthamstow 140

Gas Engines at Lambeth 142

Gate Winch from the St Katharine Docks Entrance 144

The First Television Studios 146

Remains of the Pneumatic Despatch Railway 148

Acknowledgements 150

References 153

Location Index 154

Index 160

INTRODUCTION

The first recorded mention of Londinium, 'a town of the highest repute and a busy emporium of trade and traders', occurs in the *Annals of Tacitus* compiled after the Roman Conquest in AD 43. Since then London has exercised a fascination for writers which has made it perhaps the most written-about city in the world. Even so the vast bibliography on London, which has accumulated over 2,000 years and which would appear to be all-embracing, still contains many gaps. Each year authors, scholars and researchers fill some of these, but do not, it seems, make it any more difficult for yet other groups of authors, scholars and researchers to find new and fascinating facets of this great city about which to write. The task will never be complete because London changes with the times as it has always done. New layers of history are superimposed on the old, and new plans for great and glittering futures burst forth, are acclaimed and are buried never to be resurrected. Past, present or future are all grist for the London miller.

From the tawdry booklets hawked by street traders outside hotels under foreign occupation to the lavish productions of the arty publishers, it is sufficient to indicate a taste and a subject, and the demand can be met . . . almost. You can buy guides to London Sundays, London loos, London's lost rivers or London's lovely ladies, but you cannot, it would appear, find printed directions to her vast, multifarious and unique industrial heritage—in fact to her industrial archaeology.

When this book was first proposed the term 'industrial archaeology' had not been accepted into general use and industrial archaeologists, sometimes described as 'intellectual rag-and-bone men', were neither recognized nor considered respectable.

Only 'dirt' archaeology was acceptable. But in two or three years the situation has changed beyond recognition and indeed beyond the wildest dreams of the pioneers of industrial archaeology. Since Kenneth Hudson's book *Industrial Archaeology* was published in 1963, respectability and acceptance have been thrust upon the subject and its practitioners. Indeed, 'me-too-ism' is now rife and the ultimate seal of a popular culture has been bestowed in its elevation to the Sunday colour-supplement world.

At the outset it was thought at least part of this book would have to be devoted to an explanation of industrial archaeology, its importance, and how the individual could go about helping to record or preserve items of interest. Fortunately, such an essay is now unnecessary, either as explanation or exhortation. There is an increasing sensitivity to the importance of preserving and, if not preserving, recording examples of industrial development and activity in Britain. The heritage of our industrial past belongs as much to the world as to Britain; we are merely its guardians.

A small but growing volume of studies of regions outside London is now available in published form and a concentration on single areas and industries is contributing to a total national picture. Archaeologists are desperately attempting to keep ahead of the inevitable wave of destruction which engulfs so much of value, so that to the more serious-minded it might appear to be a diversion of effort to present this random study of London's industrial relics.

The study, however, is neither as random nor as diversionary as might be thought at first glance. It is, in fact, attempting to break new ground by not following other books on industrial archaeology which have been written for the *aficionados* and by introducing to a wider audience the excitement and beauty of industrial remains and all they mean. Current studies tend to be written for the expert or presume a knowledge which may not in fact exist; very often the texts, however admirably detailed and accurate, disguise deep historical significance, catalogued descriptions hide situations of high drama, outline technical specifications conceal the roots of social change, and visual elegance is lost in the detailed engineering-type photographs.

This book is not an introduction to industrial archaeology as such. It is unashamedly a guidebook not only to where some of the physical remains of London's industrial past can be found, but also to the whole study of industrial archaeology. Professor Jack Simmons, in introducing a BBC television series on industrial archaeology, said that it is a study which can move the heart as well as the mind. This is the avowed objective of this book.

The net has been cast wide. Almost all the Standard Industrial Classifications covering manufacturing industry and many service activities are represented, and all stages of industrial development and techniques. Old construction machinery in St Paul's Cathedral is flanked by a prototype air-traffic control tower; a diorama of the 1820s is juxtaposed to a television studio of the 1930s.

The basis for the selection was not purely industrial, however. The book attempts to illustrate, through the chosen subjects, the life cycle of products from research and development through their growth to maturity, market saturation and decline, and examples of products, buildings and services in each of these stages will be found. Approaching the subject from another direction, examples have been given to illustrate the transformation of a craft to an industry, sometimes resulting in large-scale social change and indeed havoc, as can be seen in the rise and fall of the Spitalfields silk industry. Totally new structures which new industries demanded were sought, for example gasholders. Technologies have been taken at the peak of their development, a situation well illustrated by tide mills. The physical remains of an epoch now all but completely passed in Britain can be found in the remains of electric tramways, and of a minor industry dying before our eyes, the production of punched cardboard music.

Industry has not been seen simply as the manufacturing processes; a much broader view is taken and examples have been sought from the raw-material stage down to the retail outlets. Because, as is pointed out later in the book, there are no industrial goods and services which do not have as their ultimate *raison d'être* the satisfaction of some consumer wants or needs, it is not difficult to justify the inclusion of distribution and other consumer services.

A self-imposed limitation has, however, been the almost total exclusion of industrial monuments already recorded and preserved in museums, whether public or private. Items in museums are unlikely to be destroyed, whereas those on-site are subject to many and often unpredictable hazards. The temptation to include early telegraphy equipment in the private museum of Associated Electrical Industries at Woolwich, for example, was strong but nevertheless resisted. A distinction has been drawn between items such as these and others which although no longer used are preserved largely intact on-site. Sometimes the dividing line is narrow, as with the windmill at Brixton and the pumping engines at Kew Bridge.

Thus many aspects of London's industrial past and the impact on its people and their environment have been, if not probed deeply, at least identified; but not in an attempt to produce an all-embracing book. One purpose has been to show that any industry however new could, if it wished, produce its own archaeology today. Moreover, if well-meaning errors of the immediate past as well as conscious vandalism are not to lead to another holocaust of destruction, it cannot be too early to pinpoint what is valuable. 'Antiquities', said Francis Bacon, 'are history defaced, or some remnants of history which have casually escaped the shipwreck of time.' This is indeed true of so many industrial monuments and must remain true for the future unless steps are taken to make it otherwise.

All items selected, unless something completely unexpected occurs, will still exist by the time this book is published but many are unlikely to be standing or functioning before two decades have passed.

Preservation can only be attained if sufficient people care sufficiently strongly to fight for them. Thus, as a guidebook, the book has a sinister, latent purpose: to direct people to the danger spots, to inflame their emotions and move them to action. None of these objectives can be achieved unless the interesting and important facts about the subjects of this book can be explained, if needs be in emotive terms, and illustrated with a skill well beyond that of the amateur. How far the author, the researcher and the photographer fall short of this *desideratum* only the reader can say.

Preservation, however, contains within itself the seeds of its own destruction; an attempt to save everything will inevitably result in saving nothing. Reality must be faced and therefore the preservationists must be discriminating and discrimination, like statistics, is a matter of comparison. A great deal needs to be known about a great many items before an assessment can be made of their relative worth.

But why London? With the whole country to choose from, with monuments clustered from Cornwall to Caithness, then why London? The size and diversity of London is a challenge for researchers in any discipline and for industrial archaeologists it is too tempting to resist. Almost every trade and every industry, other than those depending upon natural resources not in the London area, can be found. Where else in Britain is it possible to find, within a few square miles, relics of that magnificent failure the atmospheric method of traction, evidence of candle, piano, sealing-wax, lime, bell, locomotive, veneer, silk and snuff manufacture, and a multiplicity of engineering activities? There are so many 'firsts' as to be impossible to list them all: the sub-aqueous tunnel, the container hoist, extra-high-tension electricity generation, television, gas street lighting, Portland cement and public railways.

London's industrial development is linked with the greatest names in engineering: the Brunels (father and son), Smeaton, Bramah, Stephenson (father and son), Whitworth, Telford, Boulton, Armstrong, Trevithick, Watt, Rennie. Other great pioneers abound: Ferranti, Baird, Murdoch, Barker; and its picaresque characters—Hudson, Russell and Winsor—are as interesting as its heroes, Chadwick, Waterlow, Bazalgette and Wharncliffe. London's businessmen, such as Liberty, Monsted and Whitbread, and the thousands of unknown men of genius who by invention and improvisation added substantially to the industrial heritage of London, of Britain and of the world, are also represented.

Therefore with such wealth for study London becomes well-nigh irresistible and it is more a question of how not to choose London than of why to choose it in the first place. The task of the researcher, faced with the very size and diversity of London, becomes a daunting one. Setting aside such obvious items as Tower Bridge and the Round House at Chalk Farm, systematic surveys have produced in the past little of outstanding value while all the time destruction continues unchecked. Only the demolition of such structures as the Doric Arch at Euston and the Coal Exchange attract public notice. The loss of unique examples of early clothing machinery, the breaking up of two prototype dovetailing machines and a rivet-making machine, all important in their way, have gone unchallenged.

In preparing the project upon which this book was based, a matrix was drawn up giving all Standard Industrial Classifications, followed by a major subdivision of items which are accessible to the public in one way or another and those that are not. These two major divisions were further broken down under headings: sites, machinery and buildings. This gave 144 segments. However, some industries were self-eliminating, notably the extractive industries. But there were still some

120 separate segments requiring identification if a full cross-section was to be given.

It was obvious that the usual archaeological approach, which has been facetiously described as 'turning over every stone', could never produce the diversity required to fill the matrix. Thus it was decided to attempt the process of identification by techniques common to industrial marketing research but unheard of in archaeology. A detailed description of these techniques was given by the author in a feature entitled 'Industrial Archaeology in London' in the May 1966 issue of *Industrial Archaeology, The Journal of the History of Industry and Technology*.

The various approaches adopted for the research produced nearly 400 items worthy of investigation and although many of them had either been demolished or were under threat of demolition or dismantling by the time the researchers reached them, the final problem became one of selection for the book rather than of location.

A number of criteria had to be adopted for this selection. First and obviously, that the item fell within the parameters of the study; second that it was visually interesting; and third that it bore some evidence of its original use. It was this criterion which produced perhaps the greatest problem, since many items showed little visual evidence of their original use but were nevertheless of great historical importance.

One of the most interesting finds was evidence of the remains of the first electrical generating station in the world in the basement of the Grosvenor Gallery in Bond Street, now the Aeolian Hall owned by the BBC. The walls of the basement still clearly bear traces of the generating machinery installed there, but of the machinery itself no trace remains. Also high on this list is the laboratory at Kew where viscose rayon was first developed; there is nothing in its structure or contents to indicate that it was a laboratory and so it was omitted. An early film studio at Walthamstow has been remodelled almost out of recognition, and pumping machinery at the London Hydraulic Mains Company has been modernized.

Although there was a great temptation to include what might be termed industrial oddities, these too were eliminated; for example, the dummy house in

Leinster Terrace, Bayswater, hiding the Metropolitan Railway which runs behind it, and a ventilating shaft which goes through another house at Primrose Hill. These are, to quote David Piper in his *Companion Guide to London*, 'as false as dickies, more false, to conceal the fact of life offered by the Metropolitan Railway'.

These aspects plus the proviso of life expectancy eliminated many items. Nevertheless the research brought to light examples of sites, buildings and machinery which, although not used in the book, it is to be hoped will be thoroughly investigated, photographed and recorded by industrial archaeologists in pursuit of our industrial history.

AUBREY WILSON

London
June 1967

HYDRAULIC DEVIL AT ST KATHARINE DOCKS

Although the first hydraulically-operated crane was installed in Dublin in 1804 and in 1845 William Armstrong built a quayside crane at Newcastle operated by the town water supply, it was not until 1850 that hydraulic machinery appeared at London Docks. Two pieces of early hydraulically operated mechanized cargo-handling equipment, which were developed in the transitional period of sail and steam and which have successfully survived into the twentieth century, are the hydraulic 'devils' still to be seen in daily use at 'G' Warehouse, St Katharine Docks and No. 3 Warehouse at London Docks.

Hydraulic devils, or to give them their correct name, hydraulic quay cranes, were originally installed at the docks in 1860, some ten years after the introduction of the first hydraulic equipment. Thought to be by Tannet Walker, they have a safe maximum load of 15 cwt and cost about £100 each. Originally they were on wheels and could be moved relatively easily to any part of a quay where they were needed—usually a place lacking permanent cranage.

Sailing ships without a power source to operate machinery were, in the absence of fixed quay cranes, dependent upon manually-operated capstans. With the hydraulic devil, loading and unloading could be speeded up and greater weights handled more efficiently. There was the additional advantage that they could be used to load or unload a ship not lying immediately alongside the quay but separated from it by another docked ship. While the ship nearest the quay could be discharged by fixed cranes, the devil's hauling rope could be passed across it and into the hold of the ship lying in the outer tier.

The devils are very simple mechanisms and have probably survived because of this. Water forced into the cylinder pushes out the ram which, through the chain connection to the sheaves at the top and bottom of the ram, revolves the large wheel carrying the hauling rope. The wooden cabin seen in the picture was added at a much later date to provide protection for the operators.

At the end of the last century, with the considerable extension of cranage at the quayside (electric cranes were first installed in 1890) and the passing of the sailing ship, the devils were moved to their present sites and bedded down permanently. Here they have continued to operate efficiently and economically for the last sixty years.

A TIDE MILL AT BOW

Although striking applications of steam power had been made by the end of the eighteenth century, these had by no means revolutionized industry as a whole. A great many industrial processes were not yet mechanized and even in those where power-driven machinery had been introduced, water wheels were far more numerous than steam engines and only gradually fell into disuse in the following century. Water wheels were greatly improved in efficiency and enormously expanded in size and power by millwrights and engineers such as John Smeaton and John Rennie, and later by T. C. Hewes and William Fairburn. The inventions of Thomas Savery, Thomas Newcomen and James Watt, especially the latter, have tended to overshadow these developments and it is not generally realized that water power was much more important than steam power in the early stages of the industrial revolution.[1]

The tide mill is a rare form of water mill. There were never many in number because they could only be situated at the end of, or near, the tidal flow of rivers. As the tide flowed, it would pour through the opened lock gates into the mill pond; at high tide, the gates were closed and as soon as the tide had receded sufficiently the gates were opened, the force of the returning water turning the mill wheel. Naturally the larger the millpond, the longer the mill could be worked.

The tide mill at Bromley-by-Bow, called 'Three Mills', has a long and well-documented history. Originally a remarkable group of nine mills was located on the River Lea at West Ham, three of which were a cluster of tide mills. It is obvious that by 1588 the number of mills must have been reduced, since a complaint against the occupier of Three Mills in 1588 for penning up the water at his floodgates, so that it overflowed and 'drowned' the adjoining marshes, states that 'they take in the tide at seven gates, and whereas in times past they had three mills to let it go again now they have but one corn mill and one powder mill'.[2]

In 1727 Three Mills changed from flour-milling to distilling. Later it reverted to milling, and finally in the 1890s, when it came into its present ownership, it once more became a distillery and warehouse.

The water wheels are still in position, but have been bricked up as a safety measure. The sluice, however, can still be seen.

A BRAMAH PRESS AT CHESSINGTON

Joseph Bramah is perhaps best remembered as the inventor of the hydraulic press, which was patented in 1795. The press at the Ordnance Survey offices in Chessington cannot, unfortunately, be dated, but there is little doubt that it is of early nineteenth-century manufacture, one claim actually being for 'the last decade of the eighteenth century'.

The press, which was purchased for map-production purposes, was at one time installed in the Tower of London, since map-making was the responsibility of the Army. It was moved from there to Southampton and finally came to rest in 1944 at its present home in Chessington.

The press stands $8\frac{1}{2}$ ft high, extends $3\frac{1}{2}$ ft beneath floor level and is about $4\frac{1}{2}$ ft square. The principle is that a small pump plunger is used to direct water to a ram of much larger area. Each portion of the surface of the ram equal in area to that of the plunger therefore receives a like pressure, the difference in the two total areas greatly increasing the ram pressure; a force of a few pounds acting on the pump lever is thus converted into hundreds of pounds' force at the ram.

The Ordnance Survey press exerts 1 ton pressure and is used for flattening maps or removing incorrect creases in them. It was converted from water to oil pressure and from manual to power operation in the 1930s, but the pressure remains at 1 ton. A technical feature is its glazed interleaving shelves which can be used to separate maps of different sizes into groups to avoid marking by the intermingling of small and large sheets. This interleaving also enables some maps to be withdrawn without disturbing the remainder.

The Ordnance Survey returns to Southampton in 1968 and the Bramah press must be broken up unless a new location can be found for it. If it is dismantled, an important relic and direct link with a great engineer will be lost.

DEPTFORD EAST POWER STATION

The Electrician of 9 November 1889, commenting on a visit to the Grosvenor Gallery central lighting station (now the BBC's Aeolian Hall in New Bond Street), stated:

> The installation has been regarded from the first by its promoters as experimental in character and it is here that the problems have been worked out whose successful solution has imparted that remarkable degree of confidence which is now being displayed in the far vaster undertaking at Deptford.

The demands for supply on the Grosvenor Gallery station increased so rapidly that the originators of the undertaking decided to enter a wider field. This resulted in the formation of the London Electric Supply Corporation in 1887 with £1 million capital. The immediate requirement of the company was a large generating station and a site was chosen in Deptford, at Sayes Court where the diarist John Evelyn had lived and which was later occupied by Peter the Great, who, at one time, worked as a carpenter in the nearby Royal Dockyard. The once beautiful, but long neglected, grounds were chosen by Sebastian de Ferranti as the most suitable location for his generating station because of the unlimited water supply for condensing purposes, and because seaborne coal could be procured at low prices. There was also ample space for expansion—fully used by later extensions.

Deptford was one of Ferranti's most ambitious and successful projects. It involved the transmission of electricity at extra high tension (10,000 volts) and for this reason the whole scheme was severely criticized by leading engineers in all parts of the world, including Thomas Edison who visited the station. By 1888, 1,250 hp generating units were being erected and Ferranti had plans for 10,000 hp units generating at 10 kV and with an ultimate capacity of 120,000 hp. His plans, however, were frustrated by the Board of Trade allocating much of the area which would have been supplied by Deptford to other companies. By 1889, however, 3,000 hp engines and alternators were in operation and two 5,000 hp units were being built.

A disastrous fire occurred at the Grosvenor Gallery station when it was being used as a temporary sub-station which raised doubts on the system Ferranti had adopted. In his report to the company in March 1891, Ferranti commented:

> I desire to call attention to the fact that from the commencement of your operations to the present time, no engineering or electrical difficulties whatever have arisen which I have not been able to overcome, and at the present moment I know of no weak point in your system, and consider success to be now assured. . . . The fact that current of 10,000 volts pressure is

transmitted every day to London is the most complete answer to such doubts.

The great advantage of the high pressure system is that the loss involved in the transmission of current from Deptford to the distributing station is inappreciable, while facilities for procuring coal and water there, sufficiency of room for machinery and appliances, and freedom from the legal and financial consequences attending the erection of generating stations in crowded neighbourhoods, cannot fail to tell their own tale in the working expenses of the current year.

Nevertheless, by August 1891 Ferranti had severed his relations with the London Electric Supply Corporation. He was then twenty-seven years old. The system which he had pioneered at Deptford remained in operation another forty years.[3]

It can be said that there is very little in the way of generating plant that Deptford has not pioneered. In its time, it has met a wide variety of demands, including three-phase and single-phase supplies at various frequencies. High-voltage wax-impregnated paper-insulated cables were developed for the station by Ferranti; but Deptford's main fame will undoubtedly rest on the fact that it was the first station in the world to generate and transmit electricity on extra high tension.

Although many changes have occurred, the original buildings still remain as an integral part of the present power station. The photograph shows the engine room of Ferranti's historic station, now part of the CEGB's 240 MW Deptford East Power Station. It can be seen from the early print that the original structure is largely intact.

THE FIRST THAMES TUNNEL

The Brunels, father and son, stride across nineteenth-century engineering history as giants. The genius and inventiveness of their projects and achievements are matched only by their drama and romance. None stands out more than the building of the first Thames tunnel, an incredible epic of tenacity, courage and fortitude by the Brunels, their engineers and their labourers.

When a tunnel to link north and south London was planned at the end of the eighteenth century, no sub-aqueous communication ways existed. An abortive attempt was made by Trevithick to tunnel under the Thames but was abandoned in 1808. It was only with the patenting of Marc Brunel's tunnelling method, the precursor of the modern tunnelling shield, that the possibility of the underwater link became a reality.

The work, under the direction of Marc Brunel and with his son, Isambard Kingdom Brunel, as chief engineer, commenced in 1825 with the sinking of a shaft at Cow Court on the south side of the Thames at Rotherhithe. The shaft was constructed above ground, a great cylinder of brickwork 50 ft in diameter and 42 ft high. It was so securely braced by iron tie-rods secured to cast-iron rings called 'curbs' at top and bottom that it formed a completely rigid unit. Construction began on 2 March 1825 and in three weeks the shaft reached its full height—each bricklayer laying a thousand bricks a day.

The ground was then excavated and the shaft slowly sunk at the rate of 6 inches a day. On 6 June it reached its full depth and the underpinning and removal of the iron curb commenced.

The tunnelling method adopted by Brunel was unquestionably successful but he was defeated in his early attempts both by inaccurate geological information and by pressure from the promoters of the company who insisted on doubling the safe working reach of the tunnelling shield, despite Brunel's protests. Inevitably disaster followed and the river broke into the workings three times with loss of life and considerable damage. In 1828 a new material, Portland cement, was thrown into the river in large quantities in an attempt to stop the cavity through which the water had burst. Finally, short of finance and with Britain in the depths of a depression, the work was abandoned and the directors ordered the shield to be bricked up.

Working conditions in the tunnel during its construction were appalling and throughout sickness claimed more victims than accidents. Work was conducted

WAPPING

for three years in water, and conditions were little better than in a sewer; fever and a peculiar form of tunnel sickness led to a sudden and often permanent blindness; and the immediate threat of inundation by the river hung over the whole enterprise.

The second attempt to complete the tunnel began in 1835. Conditions within the workings were now even worse; to add to the other hazards, accumulations of sewer gas produced an asphyxiating atmosphere and were always liable to ignite in flashes of flame.

Finally, in 1843, the tunnel was opened. But the original plan to include a spiral access carriageway at both ends was never carried out. Thus this project which had cost so much in life, suffering and money became only a passenger footway and something of a white elephant. It was not until 1866, when it was sold to the East London Railway Company and extended, that it was fully exploited as a north-south link. It is now part of the London Underground system.

The original tunnel is perfectly dry. The crown of the arch is so near the river bed that the throb of propellers can be heard as ships pass overhead. For nearly ninety years the fabric has been subjected to the vibration of constant railway traffic which Marc Brunel could never have envisaged, and so far as is known it has never required repair. Now over a hundred years old, the tunnel remains in its perfection a splendid tribute to its designer and builders. The shaft at Cow Court is shown in the photograph while the one at the Wapping end of the tunnel is actually part of the Underground station. The wooden staircases and their iron hand railings are the originals.[4]

TEXTILE PRINTING AT MERTON

Economic geographers have noted that London is deficient in textile manu-facture and finishing, and that evidence of any of the processes of textile produc-tion is extremely rare.[5] One example, which can still be seen, stands on the banks of the River Wandle at Merton Abbey where a calico manufactory is known to have existed since 1724 on the site of the priory. Indeed the *Victoria History of the Counties of England* notes that during the eighteenth century, along the whole course of the Wandle from Croydon to Wandsworth, and at Merton especially, 'calico printers and bleachers became well-nigh innumerable and for close upon a hundred years made this district one of the principal centres of the two industries in England'.[6]

In 1742 the buildings at Merton were occupied by William Halfhide and later by Edmund Littler. Littler printed Eastern silks for Arthur Liberty who ran the Eastern Department of Farmer & Rogers' department store in Regent Street.

Liberty played a prominent part in the Aesthetic Movement. This movement was a revulsion from the brash products of the industrial revolution, such as crude aniline dyes, machine-made finishes, false veneers, over-elaboration of products, and all the pompous ugliness of urban Victorianism. Unlike William Morris whose print works were close by, Liberty was convinced that machines could be brought to the service of art, and that the Eastern fabric weaves could be adapted to the machines of the English Midlands.

However, some of the Eastern fabrics proved too delicate or the dyes too fugitive to be made up into garments for the European market. Liberty set about persuading British manufacturers to reproduce the soft fabrics in the original Oriental and new designs, and revived some of the ancient dyeing techniques, notably those of Persia.[7] Liberty took over the Merton factory from Littler about 1885 and began handprinting both the original and new designs. He demolished many of the old weatherboarded workshops and built more substantial premises which remain largely unchanged today.

The eighteenth-century two-storey brick-colour house still stands, along with the single-storey brown-brick wheelhouse with pantile roof. An undershot iron water wheel, with four sets of spokes and hubs, has been in operation during the last twenty years. However, the bed of the Wandle was lowered in 1960 and it is unlikely the wheel will again be turned by the river.

PIANO FACTORY IN ST PANCRAS

For many years St Pancras was the London centre of the piano-manufacturing business. No one knows why St Pancras rather than anywhere else attracted piano manufacturing, but the development of the district as a great railway centre and a small but useful canal network must have been a contributing factor. Collard & Collard were undoubtedly the oldest of the well-known firms in the area. The association of Muzio Clementi with the firm ensured success since Clementi was regarded as the first genuine composer for the pianoforte. He was the idol of the salons, a friend of Mozart and Haydn and, more important in commercial terms, of many of the rich patrons of the arts.

The old Collard & Collard factory in Oval Road, St Pancras, is not, as is often thought, circular. Pevsner refers[8] to 'a circular brick building'. In fact the building is twenty-two-sectioned, for which there appears to be no specific functional or acoustical reason. Several theories exist; one is that the faceting results from the use of the standard window frames available at the time together with brick pillars of the size and strength required to support the structure, and fitting these into the available area. Another possibility is that the designers wished to provide larger areas of evenly lit working space on each floor.

The factory had five floors, and a separate manufacturing process took place on each; materials and completed components were stored at the centre while work took place around the well-lit perimeter. Between processes the pianos, either finished or partially completed, were hoisted or lowered through a large open circular well that ran from top to bottom of the building. This well is now filled in but its position and the sectional construction of the building can be seen from the photographs.

The original factory was built in 1851 and gutted by fire a year later—a hazard which removed six other piano factories in the area in the nineteenth century. Rebuilding commenced almost at once, and judging by a contemporary print showing the artist's impression of the fire the new factory closely followed the old design.

A CAPITAL PATENT CRANE IN THE CITY

Cranes were used far back in antiquity, but it is only since the industrial developments of the nineteenth century, and the introduction of motive power other than human or animal, that the crane has become indispensable. Strictly speaking the word 'crane' refers only to the arm or jib from which the load to be moved is suspended; today, however, the term is applied to the whole mechanism.

In all places where goods are handled cranes of various forms can be found. Long before this universality was achieved, and indeed when alternatives to human and animal power were still very rare, a Capital Patent Crane stood, and continues to stand, in the narrow confines of St Swithin's Lane. Of unknown age but certainly spanning a century and a half, it has remained at No. 20, occupied by Sandemans for over 150 years, in the tiny courtyard that fronts the building and just out of sight of passers-by. The original inventory of the building as taken over by George Sandeman in 1805 lists 'a Capital Patent Crane with three iron wheels, jib roller, rope pulleys and jigger'.

The mechanism is certainly not less than 160 years old and may be considerably older. The large iron wheel with its metal-to-metal braking system in fact operates both a crane and a hoist. The former carries an anchor-shaped hook on the end of the hoisting chain and was used in the courtyard for loading purposes. The hoist, which is rope-operated, is directly above the cellars.

The Capital Patent Crane is still in working order and was last called into service when the premises were damaged by bombing in 1940 and the modern lifting equipment put out of action. It was used to move stocks of vintage wine from the St Swithin's Lane vaults to safer surroundings.

ABBEY MILLS PUMPING STATION

As the vast population of London built up in the early nineteenth century, cholera became an increasing scourge. Before the work of Louis Pasteur and Robert Koch, it was believed that the contagion was spread by inhalation of a polluted atmosphere.

It was the work of Dr John Snow that proved the relationship between cholera and polluted water. In the meantime, Chadwick's historic investigation[9] had laid down the requirements of public health as being: a good water supply, the carrying away of all human waste, and the prompt removal of refuse from the streets. One of his ardent supporters, Florence Nightingale, wrote 'The true key to sanitary progress in cities is water supply and sewerage.'

Stating a solution to the hygiene problem was easier than achieving it. Mountains of refuse were heaped up at or near town centres to which was added waste from shops and privies and other noxious materials. One solution adopted in London was the appointment of 'rakers', who removed rubbish from the streets and dumped anything from which they could not make a profit in the Thames. Infected water supplies were not, however, dealt with expeditiously. It was not until 1828 that a Royal Commission recommended that all intakes of water supplies from the Thames should be moved upstream, and that suspended matter in them should be removed. These recommendations were based on aesthetic not health grounds.[10]

The general practice in the first half of the nineteenth century was to dump sewage in the nearest available river or stream and to cover in the watercourse if it became too offensive. The idea of a network of enclosed sewers independent of natural drainage channels, maintaining a steady flow of sewage towards an outfall miles away from the centre of population, was novel and apparently unrealistic.[11]

On the formation of the Metropolitan Board of Works, Joseph Bazalgette was appointed chief engineer, and by 1858 his plans for the main drainage scheme for London were approved. These included the construction of 83 miles of sewers to drain 100 square miles of the city. Bazalgette's plan had the great virtue of being radically new and so satisfactory that the sewers have needed little amendment in the hundred years since they were built. Three large new sewers on the north side of the Thames and two on the south side cross London from east to west, intercepting the old sewers on their way to the river. Thus in the Fleet, part of the water is carried off at Hampstead, at Highgate by the high-level sewer, any

excess at Kings Cross by the middle-level sewer, and the attenuated remainder by the low-level sewer at Blackfriars.[12]

The two northern low-level sewers and the Isle of Dogs branch sewer meet at the Abbey Mills Pumping Station, and the sewage and part of the storm water from the low-level system are lifted about 40 ft to the outfall sewers which lie in the embankment to the north-east side of the station. The main engine house, built between 1865 and 1868, originally housed eight beam engines with a gross capacity of about 112,000 gallons a minute. These were removed between 1931 and 1933, being replaced by eight electrically driven pumps.

The station itself has been described as 'what seems to be part of the Kremlin surrounded by trees', but the towers and cupolas add a Moorish touch to the Slavic dome. The interior has the hushed atmosphere and appearance of a Byzantine church into which, for some inscrutable and fictional reason, 'Daleks' have penetrated.

Abbey Mills has perhaps another claim to fame. John Grant, the engineer-in-charge of the London main drainage scheme, safeguarded his project by instituting tests for the cement. These were conducted on-site by machines built for the purpose. This is the first known instance of laboratory tests being carried out on-site.

GASHOLDER AT FULHAM

The emergence of the gas industry perhaps lacks the romance of the early railways, which it pre-dates by about thirty years. It has, however, its equivalent of the Stephensons and Hudson in the persons of Murdoch and Winsor.

Coal gas was at first the object of suspicion and ridicule, only a discerning few being able to realize the possibilities that lay behind this remarkable discovery. Walter Scott wrote to a friend in Scotland that there was 'a madman proposing to light London with—what do you think? Why, with smoke.'[13]

Murdoch lit his office in Redruth with gas in 1792 and Winsor demonstrated the first public lighting along the garden wall of Carlton House in 1807. In 1812 a Charter was granted for the Gas Light & Coke Company to supply gas to London, Westminster, Southwark and the adjacent suburbs. By 1816 gas was common in London, and by 1819 gasworks were in operation throughout the country. A committee of the Royal Society which visited gasworks in Peter Street noted that there was but one gasholder with a capacity of 15,000 cu. ft, but by 1822 it contained eighteen gasholders, averaging 15,000 cu. ft each.

In the early days of gas manufacture, the gasholder was made to serve the purpose of a gas measurer by the addition of a scale of feet and inches, so that the depth of gas in the vessel, multiplied by its area, gave the cubic content. Thus the term 'gasometer' was coined.

From the beginning of gas manufacture, it was found advantageous to provide a reserve store and this was best achieved in the bulky gasholders. A gasholder consists essentially of a large cup or bell sealed in a tank of water, the bell being floated by the gas, and rising or falling as it is stored or withdrawn. The bell is located centrally in the tank by vertical guides mounted on columns built round the tank. Gasholders can be designed in more than one section, the sections interlocking and lifting and descending telescopically.

The No. 2 holder at Fulham in the photograph was built in 1830, the year of Winsor's death, and is reputed to be the oldest working holder in Britain, if not in the world. It is a single-lift water-sealed holder in a below-ground brick tank. The diameter is 100 ft with a lift weight of 30 ft and a gas storage capacity of 234,000 cu. ft.

VENEER LATHE IN MILE END

Like so many crafts which later became industries, the production of veneers dates back to the ancient world. Ancient Egypt, Chaldea and Assyria in their various civilizations were capable of efficient veneering. Later, in the Middle Ages, intersia and marquetry work which are closely allied to and dependent upon the art of veneer production developed. Changing tastes in decoration and increasing affluence stimulated a considerable demand for veneers of all types which could not be met from the laborious hand methods of production.

In the usual process of veneer manufacture, the 'flitches' (slices of timber from a tree trunk) were steamed before being cut, and the sheet thus obtained carefully dried. Veneers could be cut at many different angles to the grain and growth rings of a tree, producing varying patterns and interesting effects. Human skills of veneer production were, and are, as much connected with maximum utilization of the log as with the careful matching and application of patterns.

By the middle of the nineteenth century, mechanical methods of production had developed, one of which was the veneer lathe. The essential principle of all lathes is the rotation on a shaft of the work to be turned and the application of a cutting tool to the revolving object. In ordinary rotary-cut veneer, it is most economical to select logs which are as near cylindrical as possible, because until the log has been reduced to a cylinder it cannot be peeled off in a complete sheet. A log is suspended horizontally between two chucks and rotated against a knife. The veneer is peeled off and reeled for storage. It is later unreeled and clipped into sheets.

With most species, the log has to be steamed or boiled before peeling so that the timber is really hot and moist when it is put on the machine. In order to rotate a log of perhaps up to 3 or 4 tons and to withstand constant moisture and heat while producing a veneer which may not differ in thickness more than a few thousandths of an inch, the lathe not only has to be a precision instrument but of extremely robust construction.

John Wright & Sons in Mile End have a very early veneer lathe, designed by John Wright himself and manufactured by a local engineer *circa* 1866. It was used continually until 1922 and has now been preserved and mounted on the roof of their building. This lathe is said to be one of the very first mechanical veneer peelers.

CONTROL TOWER AT CROYDON AIRPORT

For the old and middle-aged, the name Croydon evokes the thrill of the early days of flying, when a passing aeroplane had necks craning for a glimpse of it, while to witness a landing or take-off was an event to be talked of for days. Even vicariously, Croydon cast its spell of adventure everywhere through the heroes and heroines of its heyday—Jim Mollison, Amy Johnson, Charles Lindberg, Charles Scott, Tom Campbell-Black, A. E. Clouston and Betty Kirby-Green. Croydon was the start or finish of many record-breaking flights.

The first Croydon aerodrome was established by the Royal Flying Corps in 1915 and was used for training and the defence of London in World War One. A government-owned National Aircraft Factory was also built on the site. In 1920 Croydon became London's main civil airport and by 1924 Imperial Airways, later to become BOAC, was based there. In 1927–28 the airport buildings were re-constructed and officially opened on 2 May 1928.

The terminal at Croydon was the most advanced of its kind and for a number of years was one of the largest and most completely equipped airport buildings in the world. Within it were incorporated, besides traffic control, the administrative offices of the airport, airline offices and also provisions for passenger handling, freight, immigration and customs. Restaurant and hotel accommodation was provided at the nearby Airport Hotel which still functions within the airport bounds.

During World War Two, the airport reverted to a fighter station and later to transport use. After the war, short-haul domestic and European routes were operated from Croydon, but because the aerodrome could not be further developed, after a period of serving charter and civil users, it was finally closed in 1957. The terminal buildings are now used for commercial offices.

The control towers of today may be taller and glassier but they still retain something of the original functional shape pioneered at Croydon.

SEWER-GAS LAMP OFF THE STRAND

The first experiments in gas street lighting took place in Golden Lane in the City of London, in 1807, and the City of Westminster was the first authority in the world to light a public street, Pall Mall, by gas in 1812. By 1823 there were nearly 40,000 public gas lamps, lighting 215 miles of London's streets.

Although today an era is drawing to its close, as late as 1958 it was still possible for a recognized authority on public lighting to make a plea on economic and technical grounds for the continued use of gas lighting in certain types of streets.[14] With the promise of abundant supplies of cheap natural gas, gas lighting may still hold its attraction in areas where conversion has not taken place or is scheduled.

Obviously, however, redevelopment and urban renewal will remove or convert most of the existing gas lamps to electricity; but the City of Westminster intends to preserve a unique gas lamp in Carting Lane off the Strand. This is a Webb 'Patent Sewer Lamp', of which no other example survives in London.

In 1895 J. E. Webb patented a street-lighting column which combined its purpose of illumination with that of sewer gas extraction and destruction. Over 2,500 of these lamps were sold throughout the world. A few remain in Britain today, notably outside London, in Sheffield, Whitley Bay and Blyth. The one in Carting Lane is a particularly fine example. The lamp was installed in 1900 to dispose of gases arising from the drains near the Savoy Hotel. It was originally fitted with flat, plain, fish-tail burners but was later converted to the incandescent type.

The lamp operates on town gas, not sewer gas as has been mistakenly thought. A tube which passes through the lamp column from the sewer below carries sewer gas to the flames where all the impurities are burned.

The fluted iron column with its richly ornamented lantern is a particularly handsome specimen of street furniture, according well with its surroundings.

RELICS FROM THE PRE-HISTORY OF RAILWAYS

The opening of the Surrey Iron Railway marks a most important stage in transport history. It was the first public railway in the world, pre-dating the more famous Liverpool–Manchester line by a quarter of a century, and was the first line of any kind in the south of England. The Surrey Iron Railway Company was incorporated under an Act of 21 May 1801, and William Jessop, part-owner of the Butterley Iron Works, was appointed engineer. Members of the public could use their own horses and wagons over the company's lines on payment of tolls which were eventually set at a maximum of 6d per ton mile.

The Surrey Iron Railway was conceived as part of a route, comprising both canals and railways, between London and Portsmouth; transport of heavy goods was presenting great difficulties on the existing rough and inadequate roads. Part of the impetus behind the construction of the line was the necessity to send supplies to Portsmouth for the fleet engaged in battles against Napoleon.

The double track was laid with plate rails on stone sleepers. The rails were grooved to guide the wheels of the wagons, flanged wheels not having been developed at that time.

A second company was formed in 1803—the Croydon, Merstham & Godstone Railway Company—which undertook to extend the Surrey Iron Railway up the dry valley south of Croydon to the Merstham gap in the North Downs, and then on to Reigate and Portsmouth. The high cost of construction and Nelson's victories removed the urge to press on to Portsmouth and indeed even to Reigate. The line never reached beyond the Greystone lime works at Merstham.

Now a series of footpaths and rights-of-way, the route of the extended single track can still be traced with little difficulty along the side of the valley opposite that of the Brighton line.[15]

Both railways were unsuccessful, mainly due to the adoption of Wandsworth as the chief terminus.[16] The Croydon, Merstham & Godstone line was closed in 1838, followed by the Surrey Iron Railway in 1846.

Relics of both lines in the form of stone sleepers in rockeries and walls of gardens can still be found along the route. Sections of re-laid track exist at Purley Rotary Field and in the grounds of Wallington Public Library. The photograph shows the section of fish-bellied track outside the Joliffe Arms Hotel on the A23 Brighton Road.

AN OLD HAND-PRINTING PRESS AT FINSBURY PARK

It is generally accepted that the Chinese were the first printers; there is no certainty as to the actual date of the European invention of printing from movable type, but it is believed to have been about 1440; nor is there any certainty about to whom the invention of printing from movable type can be attributed, or where it took place. A printing press at Mainz in Germany ascribed to Johann Gutenberg is usually regarded as the first of the genre; certainly Caxton, who introduced printing into England, learnt his craft in Germany.

The development of the printing press provides a remarkable history of achievement. Wooden hand-operated machines working on a screw principle were first used as early as 1570 and remained largely unchanged until the end of the eighteenth century. The advance then made was to substitute a series of compound levers for the screw. The hand-lever press, operating on the toggle-jointed bar principle, eventually superseded all others; this type was made in London from about 1817.

The printing press which is lovingly preserved and still used for pulling proofs at Hunnings Printers Ltd, in Finsbury Park, bears the legend 'Improved Hercules Press', and the date 1845; it was manufactured by J. Smith, Denmark Street, Soho. Above the date are the figures '6' and '3' which may refer to the day and month of completion. It provides a direct link with the early days of the hand-lever machine.

A wooden sub-base about 2 ft high carries the press which consists of a bed on which the block of print is placed. The print is inked with a roller and paper placed on top. A handle winds the bed under the frame of the press. A lever then operates a cam to bring down the pressure plate which presses the paper on to the print. The lever is then raised and the bed wound clear for the removal of the paper and replacement by a new sheet.

The balanced operation of the handle is exceptional and shows considerable skill in design and construction. Indeed the press could be operated all day and at a high rate without undue fatigue. It is designed for foolscap printing and is completely unmodified, showing no signs of needing repair. The cast-iron frame is joined by wedges and bolts, and has the old type of square nuts.

AN UMBRELLA SHOP IN HOLBORN

There is no demand for industrial goods and services which does not ultimately stem from a demand for consumer goods and services. All the objects illustrated and described in this book depended for their profitable use upon consumer demand. Thus retailing fits into the pattern of industrial activity as appropriately as machine tools.

Older shops than the one in Holborn belonging to James Smith & Sons, umbrella and walking-stick specialists, can be found without difficulty. Smith's, however, is a perfect example of a late Victorian shop, complete in every detail. Victorian Renaissance above and Gothic ironwork below, it is decorated with an abundance of ornamental lettering.[17] An engraved brass stallboard underneath the window bears the legend 'James Smith & Sons, Umbrella Warehouse and Stick Factory' and below this is a glass-faced plinth lettered in black, red and gold with the capital letters ornamented by flower decorations. Exterior, fascia and interior have all remained largely unchanged for over 100 years. Inside the only obvious alteration has been the removal of some of the Victorian show-cases to provide more space.

Originally there was only one fairly small shop but as the adjoining premises became vacant so they were taken over. The building itself is in fact pre-Victorian, *circa* 1800, and is held on a Crown lease. The Smith family appears to have opened the shop about 1850. Certainly the Holborn Borough Council had dealings with the family at this date.

Considerable effort has been needed, of course, to preserve the original appearance of the shop. The windows re-glazed after war damage are almost identical with the originals. More serious damage occurred in 1966 when a vehicle collided with the building, damaging the fascia and lettering, but once again it was found possible to restore the shop-front to its original appearance. However, little remains of the white porcelain lettering, once so common in all shops.

The Victorian retailer's custom of detailing on his shop-front as much as possible of the wares available inside is well illustrated. Thus the Smith's fascia, apart from announcing the building's name 'Hazlewood House', and displaying a White Ensign and Star-Spangled Banner above the door to support the legend 'English and American Umbrella and Stick Store', lists at some length offers of riding crops and whips, Irish blackthorns, Malacca canes and other stock items.

POTTERY KILN IN KENSINGTON

If the clay soil of Notting Hill made it unsuitable for horse-racing and closed the short-lived Hippodrome Racecourse at Kensington within five years, it certainly favoured brick-making, and a number of small potteries are also known to have existed in the area. A picture of the Hippodrome Racecourse by Henry Aiken (1842) clearly shows a kiln in the background, and an 1847 survey of the Parish of St Mary Abbots indicates the location of 'potteries' and 'pottery sheds' in sufficient number for the district to have acquired the name of its principal trade—'the Potteries'.

In *Household Words* (1850) Charles Dickens wrote:

> In a neighbourhood studded thickly with elegant villas and mansions, viz. Bayswater and Notting Hill, in the parish of Kensington, is a plague spot, scarcely equalled for its insalubrity by any other in London; it is called the Potteries.

Charles Booth, in his *Life and Labour of the People of London* (1904), stated that the inhabitants of the district were 'criminal and irreclaimable'.

All potteries need considerable supplies of raw material so that it is not surprising to find in an early record of Notting Hill that a 'brickfield of yellow clay, covering some 17 acres' was leased to a pottery in 1781. This site is now covered by Walmer Road, Portland Road and an area to the north of Holland Park Avenue.

It has been inferred[18] that many of the Kensington potteries manufactured, glazed and painted, or transfer-decorated, wall tiles. The manufactory at Hippodrome Place (off Portland Road), of which the kiln illustrated is all that remains, existed in the mid-nineteenth century and was producing flower pots, drain pipes and similar articles. The kiln is now built into a wall surrounding an existing factory. It is about 36 ft high with a 15-ft diameter at the base, rising conically to a 3-ft diameter at the top. Although the inside of the kiln is now clogged with masonry and rubbish, its exterior is in reasonably good condition.

A NINETEENTH-CENTURY PLANING MACHINE IN ELTHAM

Several engineers, such as Matthew Murray of Leeds, James Fox of Derby and Richard Roberts of Manchester, appear independently to have produced metal-planing machines in the second decade of the nineteenth century.

One of the most famous names in nineteenth-century engineering is that of Joseph Whitworth, who established himself in Manchester in the early 1830s. His company achieved an immense reputation for machine tools, armaments and precision engineering by using, for example, true plane surfaces and accurate measurement, and standardizing screw threads.[19] A photograph of the Whitworth factory in 1866 at Chorlton Street, Manchester, apart from contrasting strongly in orderliness with other works of the time, shows machines similar to the planing machine illustrated, which is still operating for Walter Grafton & Son Ltd, Eltham.

There is little doubt that when Whitworths delivered Planing Machine No. 623 they did not expect it to be in use, and still accurate to $\pm0\cdot001$ inch over table area, seventy years or more later. This is a typical example of the superb quality of workmanship and materials used by the best machine-tool builders of the mid-nineteenth century.

The machine operates by the workpiece which is firmly bolted to a sliding table, travelling backwards and forwards under the cutting tool, which can be lowered and adjusted to cut more or less deeply. The planer is belt-driven, 3 ft by 2 ft, with split nut and screw table drive. The table has twin 'V' slides with adjustable reversing 'dogs' with fast return. Cross and vertical slides can be power operated and the latter can be angled at 40° in either direction.

Originally thought to have been sold to the famous tool and cutter makers, Arthur Martin & Company of Westcombe Park, London, the machine came to Walter Grafton & Son in the early 1900s. Some adjustments have been made to the original design, but its continued accuracy and efficiency have justified the cost of bringing it more into line with today's practices. A surface grinding attachment replaces the original tool box and a hydraulic power unit has been installed in the last few years.

A CANDLE FACTORY IN BATTERSEA

Candles must be among the oldest of all the objects referred to in this book and have probably remained visually, if not chemically, almost unchanged for over 2,000 years. It might have been thought that the vast changes in technology in lighting would have spelled the demise of the candle, except for symbolic purposes, hundreds of years ago. The oil lamp, gas and electricity each in their turn provided better forms of illumination. Nevertheless, at the time of the 1958 Census of Production output of candles was worth almost £6 million.

The candle mould, a French invention, consisted of a wooden frame with metal tubes set in it and a simple device for holding the wicks stretching through the centre of the moulds. This type of mould is still in use for making candles of special shapes and sizes. Moulding, however, made little progress until the harder materials, such as spermaceti and stearine, came into use. (Stearine was preferred by explorers, since it could be used in an emergency to supplement food supplies.) From here on, the new inventions appear to have been British. In 1801 Thomas Binns of Marylebone patented an improved mould using water cooling, and Joseph Morgan of Manchester produced a machine that enabled candles to be removed from the moulds with greater ease and facilitated continuous wicking. Joseph Tuck and William Palmer of London invented a clamp for holding the candles after their release and a mechanism for ejecting them from the moulds. The incorporation of these and other improvements into the prototype of the modern candle-making machine was, however, due to two Americans, John Stainthorp and Willis Hummiston.

Price's Patent Candle Company, part of whose plant is illustrated, began as a partnership in 1830. By 1848 they employed over 700 people in their factory at Vauxhall covering nearly two acres. By 1860 the company had moved to Battersea, where they today occupy over ten acres.

Although the factory contains mostly modern machinery, evidence of the older methods exists. Some church candles are still manufactured by hand because of the vast range of often non-standard expensive candlesticks and candelabra in use in churches. The process consists of pouring and building up layer upon layer of bees'-wax, the wicks being hung on wooden rings before the pouring is started, as can be seen in the bottom right-hand corner of the photograph.

COAL DUTY POSTS

From time immemorial, the Corporation of London acted as bailiff and supervised the conservancy of the River Thames, also acting as measurer of, among other things, all coals brought into the Port of London. After the Great Fire of 1666 the City Corporation had a net deficiency of £240,000, and probably suggested taxing coal to help put their finances in order. Coal was in wide use and in view of its bulk difficult to 'smuggle'.

The first yield—about £10,000 annually—was directed to making good some of the damage caused by the fire and also for widening streets and rebuilding wharves and prisons. In 1834, with the debts paid off, the duty yielded was directed to Metropolitan improvements which included Moorgate, the approaches to London Bridge, Cheapside, Aldersgate, the Victorian, Chelsea and Albert Embankments, Hyde Park Corner and the northern and southern sewage outfalls.

When the transport of much coal changed from the sea to inland navigation routes the tax became more difficult to collect. Thus, the first boundary markers appeared in 1805 just north of Watford and at Staines, indicating the point at which duty became payable. Boundaries were first set at twenty-five miles from the London GPO headquarters and later reduced to twenty miles.

An Act of 1861 authorized the setting up of hundreds of boundary markers where any canal, inland navigation, railway turnpike or public road first entered the Metropolitan Police district. At that time, duties consisted of 4s per tun on wine and 1d per ton on coals, culm and cinders.[20]

There were seven different types of marker posts—obelisks of varying shapes in stone or cast-iron, square-shaped cast-iron posts and cast-iron plaques. The example in the photograph is situated at Rickmansworth. Although all the posts have not been recorded, there were at one time over 250 and they are not difficult to locate: in the north and north-east planning area of Surrey alone, fifty-four are listed.

The various Acts relating to duties on goods entering London were rescinded in 1889, and the rights of the Corporation of London to collect tolls on coal and to act as weighers and measurers of coal finally expired in 1890.

24&25VICT
CAP 42

BENE

WATER-METER TESTING TOWER AT ISLINGTON

While man was emerging from the pre-civilized state of self-sufficiency as hunter of his food, maker of his clothing and builder of his own rude shelter, he began to specialize in elemental crafts such as making tools and weapons, growing crops, domesticating animals, weaving, crude carpentry, pottery and working metals.

Over a very long period of time and from these primitive beginnings rose the necessity for means to measure, both for the purpose of barter and to enable crafts to develop. The oldest concept would naturally have been that of length, followed by the appreciation of two-dimensional area and of three-dimensional bulk. The abstract idea of weight probably took longer to dawn on early man's intelligence. Weighing with balances is certainly among the really fundamental inventions of prehistoric times.

As crafts and commerce developed, new methods and new skills of measurement accompanied them. The Industrial Revolution created a demand for control and for instrumentation, particularly for the power sources—water, steam, gas and later electricity. The further technology advanced, the more urgent became the need for accurate measurement. This in turn implied that measuring devices had themselves to be subject to rigid performance standards.

Tylor's, established in 1787, was the first firm to produce water-metering devices on a large scale. These were of the inferential or fan type; improved versions using this principle are still made. Later a rotary piston displacement type was patented which is still today the most widely accepted method of operation for meters required to satisfy exacting conditions. In order to test and calibrate the meters, it was necessary to have large quantities of water at known and constant pressures. This was achieved in 1870 by setting three water tanks at different heights in a tower some 150 ft high on the site of the Tylor factory at Belle Isle near Kings Cross.

The structure of the tower shows the position of the main tank at a height of about 100 ft. This gave a static pressure of 50 lb per sq in. In addition, inside the brickwork were two smaller tanks at lower levels, giving pressures of 20 lb and 10 lb respectively. A large flue passed through an aperture in the three tanks; this served the double purpose of providing a draught for the boilers producing power for the factory, and ensuring that the tanks did not freeze up in winter. The outlet of the flue can still be seen at the top of the tower.

The tanks were connected to test beds in the factory and all sizes of meters could be tested and calibrated at three different pressures. After passing through the meters, the water was fed into calibrated tanks and when the readings had been taken it was discharged into a storage tank under the factory floor, then pumped back up to the tower tanks again. By re-use, waste of public water supplies was avoided. Fundamentally the same principle is used for testing water meters today and a somewhat more modest water tower is part of the present Tylor factory at Burgess Hill.

It is said that two construction firms were bankrupted in the process of preparing the foundations for the tower at Belle Isle, which must have proved more difficult than had been foreseen.

After World War Two it was found that German Air Force maps had pinpointed the tower as an identification aid for the nearby railway marshalling yards. Today it remains as a landmark and still functions as a boiler flue for the factory, now occupied by a plastics manufacturer.

CONTAINER HOIST IN CLERKENWELL

The container principle of freight movement is now a vital and increasingly important part of the logistics of industry, used for motor vehicles, ships, aircraft and trains. In this last instance, it is the core of the much-vaunted British Rail liner-train system of transportation.

The first experiment in container transport, begun as early as 1914 by the firm of Carter Paterson, took place at the Central Street, City Road depot, next to the Macclesfield Road Parcels Depot—itself built on the historic site of the City Basin where barges were once unloaded. The system was not completed until 1919, when it was considered to be employing the most advanced equipment of its type in the country, if not in the world.

The purpose of the container system was to permit greater utilization of vehicles by shortening the turn-round period at the depot. Goods were loaded in containers which in turn were mounted on flat lorries. As soon as these arrived at the depot, the containers would be lifted off by a crane and dropped on to 'shelves' or on to the loading bay. A filled container would be mounted on the lorry which could then leave; about 15 minutes became the usual turn-round period.

The installation at the City Road Depot of British Road Services was manufactured by Herbert Morris of Loughborough. It comprises two conventional three-motor DC 5-ton overhead electric travelling cranes on a steel gantry/runway, travelling above the loading bays. The cranes are about 30 ft from the ground, and at 15 ft above ground level on the opposite side to the loading bays is the steel 'shelf' covering half the traverse of the cranes. The lifting arrangements include spreader beams with four hooks at the corners for lifting the road containers; there is also a centre hook for lifting railway containers. The hook of one of the cranes is suspended from a circular turntable which can be turned by a fourth motor on the crane, so that containers may be rotated after lifting.

The cranes straddled the incoming containers which were then lifted above the decking and moved down to a vacant unloading bay, to rest on wooden trestles. If, however, the container was to be stored, the crane would deposit it on the 'shelf'.

The system was in full operation until about 1955 when it became obsolete on the introduction of articulated trailers. It is, however, still used occasionally.

A COLD ROLLING MACHINE AT BROMLEY-BY-BOW

During the nineteenth century, iron and steel were required in ever-increasing quantities for machinery, constructions and a whole host of products either new in themselves or being made with iron and steel for the first time. Not surprisingly, great technical improvements were made to facilitate the production both of metals and of the items made from them. Machine tools increasingly displaced manual labour.

One example of this was the cold rolling machine, used to flatten mild-steel plates which had twisted and warped in storage. The plates were rolled from red-hot ingots of steel in the rolling mill of a steel works, and suffered from built-in stresses caused by the outside of the plate cooling first; these stresses led to warping, so that the plate had to be flattened before it was used. Before the advent of the cold rolling machine, a plater had to note the twists and point out their position to a labourer, who then hit the plate with a 14-lb sledge hammer.

The cold rolling machine at the Ratner Safe Company works was made by Craig & Donald, Glasgow, and was installed about 1891 when the present Ratner works were built. It was designed to straighten mild-steel plates up to $\frac{1}{2}$ in thick, although it could in fact operate on slightly thicker plates. The machine has seven solid steel rollers 5 ft 6 in long and of 9 in diameter, arranged in two layers, four above and three below. The top rollers, aligned to the gaps between the bottom rollers, can be raised and lowered by a hand-wheel—three of them together by the large wheel on the right of the photograph, and the fourth, on the feed-in side, independently.

The plate for flattening is fed in at one end, the rotating rollers driving it through to the other end where it is reversed. If the pressure on the rollers is correctly adjusted, the plate is completely flat after the reverse movement through the machine, although a badly twisted plate may need two or three passes.

Ratner's machine is still used after over seventy-five years' work. The only modification has been the conversion from line shafting to an independent motor drive; also, as safety regulations have tightened, some protective fencing has been added.

THE 'ROUND HOUSE' AT CHALK FARM

One of the most familiar, if unremarked, sights to north Londoners travelling to the centre of the City by road, or to train passengers gathering up their belongings as the train slows at Chalk Farm before entering Euston Station, is a circular building with a conical roof. For nearly one hundred years it was one of Gilbeys' bonded warehouses and is now the first home of Centre 42, Arnold Wesker's cultural mausoleum. Originally, however, it was an engine shed of unusual design.

Contrary to the general belief that the 'Round House' was built to enable trains to be hauled by cable from Euston to Camden (this practice ceased in 1844 on the introduction of more powerful locomotives), the shed was designed and built for housing engines and general repair work.

The 'Round House' was commissioned in 1846 by the London & Birmingham Railway Company. There are conflicting views as to who actually designed the building. An agreement, signed 11 June 1846, states that Robert Benson Dockray, then engineer to the London & Birmingham Railway Company, 'prepared a specification and plans, sections and drawings of the various works'. The Stephensons are always closely associated with the building and in several books they are referred to as the designers, but the evidence seems to suggest that their role was that of consultants.

The area of the 'Round House' is approximately 2,234 sq. yd, and it is 180 ft in diameter. The iron roof is carried on twenty-four cast-iron columns and it has been assumed that there were twenty-four tracks running between the columns emanating from the centre of the building, where a turntable and a pit enabled clinker to be removed more easily and general repairs to be carried out. If this is correct, then twenty-four engines could have been housed at one time. The circular form of the building rendered every engine easily accessible and quickly removeable.

Some of the original tracks remain, let into the floor. Beneath the buildings is a honeycomb of tunnels, now filled with debris, but once giving access to the inspection pits and allowing the removal of clinker.

FOOD-DRYING KILNS IN LAMBETH

The oast house is usually associated with Kent, and certainly with the countryside, so that it comes as a visual surprise to find two of the typical conical roofs, but without their traditional cowls and vanes, surmounting brick-built kilns in the heart of Lambeth. Their connection with the Kentish oast house is, however, direct and logical.

Thomas Dence, the founder of Brand & Co. Ltd, was a Kentish man. When his firm required a food-drying installation, it was perhaps natural that his ideas should turn to the highly efficient oast houses which so effectively dried the Kentish hops. Brand's Essence, long a household name, and which incidentally succeeded viper broth as a popular invalid food, is extracted from beef and chicken. After extraction, the meat is then suitable only for animal food. Before it can be processed for this purpose it must be thoroughly dried.

The beef and chicken, with the essence extracted, were cut into about one-inch cubes and taken to the second floor of the Lambeth building by a hand-operated lift. Here the cubes were spread over an iron open-mesh floor, beneath which a wood fire was lit. The conical roofs induced a strong upward draught which, to some extent, was controlled by limiting the access of air to the lower floors.

One of the hazards of this drying process was that the fat would frequently drip into the fire and ignite, so that before long the fire was out of control. Apparently it was a commonplace occurrence to call the fire brigade to douse the fire as often as once or twice a month. The total drying process took about 24 hours, compared with today's rate of $1\frac{1}{2}$ hours for up to $2\frac{1}{2}$ tons of meat.

The kilns, made from London stock brick, were erected about 1900 and have survived London weather, the vibration of the Southern Region's main line which runs close by, and flying and incendiary bombs within yards. Today the building is no longer part of the food-drying plant but is still in use, to some extent for its original purpose. Apart from storage, some incineration takes place there, the conical roofs continuing to provide the strong upward draughts needed for quick burning.

Oast houses have been accurately described as constituting architecture of pure geometry; it is perhaps not remarkable, therefore, that they fit as snugly into the industrial landscape of Lambeth as into the Kentish countryside.[21]

HERMITAGE INNER CUTTING SWING BRIDGE, LONDON DOCKS

The Hermitage basin at the London Docks was opened in 1811 but was not cut through to the Thames until 1821. Originally two bridges crossed the basin: an outer one—the public road—and an inner one—the dock road. The inner cutting swing bridge in the photograph was not frequently operated nor heavily employed by land traffic since the basin itself was seldom used, even in the nineteenth century. Nevertheless, the fact that it continues to serve troublefree after approaching 150 years and to carry axle loads up to 4 tons is a tribute to the skill of its designers and builders.

It is one of the last pieces of work by John Rennie, Senior, who died in 1821. A letter of 25 July 1820 from Rennie refers to it and somewhat poignantly highlights the problem of the basin construction:

> I beg leave to observe that I have used every means in my power to urge the respective contractors forward on the works at Hermitage Basin and generally speaking I have found them ready to meet my wishes. Several causes may be assigned for the noncompletion of the works by mid-summer last. First, long continuation of the winter, second, very little space to deposit material. Thirdly, the great and I may say almost unprecedented trouble in keeping the sewer which runs along the west side of the lock from breaking into the work. Fourthly, the shoring up and keeping of the buildings on each side. And, lastly, and principally, a great delay has been occasioned by the non-completion of the new road over the swivel bridge.

The bridge is made with enormously thick cast-iron ribs. A similar bridge, over the Wapping cutting to the east, was broken up in 1954 and the cast-iron was found to be in magnificent condition. There were no blow holes even though the ribs were 2 in thick and the wrought-iron tie-bars between the ribs had sharp angles on them. The square bars were very heavily crystallized and on fracture they looked like pieces of silver.

Originally hand-operated, the bridge was converted to electric drive in 1918, the motor being geared to the original hand-operated winch. Although only opened occasionally to allow a dredger into the basin, it still works smoothly, quietly and with astonishing speed.

MARGARINE FACTORY IN SOUTHALL

Margarine was patented by a French scientist, Mège-Mouriez, who in 1870 during the Siege of Paris, working on a false hypothesis, made 'butter fat' from a mixture of milk and beef fat as a substitute for butter which he called oleo-margarine. His process set off the rapid development of the industry. Gradually animal fats were replaced by vegetable fats as a result of improvements in the hydrogenization process. Margarine achieved immediate popularity among the poorer classes and indeed in its own way created a minor revolution in eating habits as well as stimulating trade in many poor tropical countries because of the demand for copra for its production.

When margarine was first introduced into Denmark, its manufacture was taken up by Otto Monsted. As the Danish market became saturated, Monsted looked further afield and by 1889 was producing margarine in an old hat factory at Goldey near Hyde in Cheshire. The demand rapidly outpaced the factory's capacity so that in 1893 Monsted purchased land between the Grand Junction Canal and the Great Western Railway at Southall for a new model factory. It was designed by Bird & Whittenbury of Manchester, and built in sturdy red brick by A. B. Hanson of Southall. Its Dutch style has a suggestion of baroque. The timber roof trusses of the original warehouse are of geodetic construction and were unique for their time. The original wrought-iron gates have *art nouveau* decoration.

The site was totally independent of public services; DC electricity was generated, water was pumped from three wells, and the site had its own narrow-gauge railway and private waterway, including a basin and covered docks. The factory also raised its own steam, had a fully-equipped laundry and, unusual in its day, a complete air-conditioning plant.

By 1912 the Monsted factory covered 56 acres, employed nearly 1,000 men and women, and had a productive capacity of $3\frac{1}{2}$ million pounds of margarine a week. 'It is fitted with the latest and finest machinery and can in every way substantiate its claim to be the largest and finest margarine factory in the world.'[22]

At a time when official supervision of hygiene was not as stringent as today and public demand for safeguards not as insistent, the Monsted factory was a model of cleanliness and good order. All surfaces in contact with the margarine were of aluminium as far as possible; absolute cleanliness was insisted on in the white-tiled rooms, their floors continually awash. The latest handling, processing

and packaging equipment was installed, all it seems without labour or demarcation troubles.

> If anyone wanted definitive and conclusive proof that the invention of labour-saving machinery is one of labour's greatest friends, here truly is an instance. . . . Where profit-sharing is in vogue, as it is in the Monsted factories, the workmen are themselves only too anxious to fall in with new schemes, and suggestions for labour-saving devices and inventions have been made by the workmen themselves.[23]

Staff welfare figured highly in Monsted's complex and he was well in advance of his time with fringe and other benefits. A large works institute had a fully equipped stage, cinema projection room, bar, cellar and Canadian maplewood floor for dancing and roller skating. The institute also contained a library and reading rooms, a rifle range, a racquet court and a skittle alley. Whether conditions were as idyllic as the physical amenities might indicate cannot be said, but certainly Monsted was not only a technical innovator but also genuinely concerned with his social responsibilities as an employer.

When the Margarine Union was formed in 1927, production was transferred to Van den Burgh's factory in Fulham. The great complex was closed and the production machinery torn out. Various parts of the estate were sold off while the main plant remained empty until 1932, after which a succession of food-manufacturing firms occupied it; all of them are now part of the Unilever group.

AN ETHER PLANT AT ILFORD

To the lay public at least, the development of anaesthesia has been the most important single advance in medicine. In 1818 Michael Faraday discovered that ether vapour, like nitrous oxide, had anaesthetic properties. The phenomenon produced by these two gases remained a curiosity, however, until 1842, when an American, Dr Crawford Long, performed an operation under ether. In Britain the first recorded use was in 1846 by a London dentist and a few days later by Robert Lister, the eminent surgeon.

Today throughout the world ether is still used more often than other anaesthetics. More sophisticated equipment developed over the last few years allows the use of other gases, but none are as easy to administer and control or as cheap as ether.

The ether plant shown in the photograph is at the works of Howards, established in Stratford as early as 1797. The plant cannot be dated exactly but a study of the threads, materials and general construction leads to the conclusion that it was probably built between 1895 and 1910.

The plant is in three rooms, the first containing three lead vats of approximately 3 ft 6 in diameter with domed tops and holding approximately 150 gallons each. Each vat has a stirrer operated through a shaft drive and bevel gears by a motor located outside the building in order to avoid the risk of fire or explosion. The first stage of ether production is carried on in these vats, after which the liquor is conveyed into stills in the second room. These are large iron vessels fitted with a lead steam-heating coil and large copper stacks leading through the roof. After boiling in the stills the distillate passes into the third room to water-cooled lead vats and a brine-cooled tank for final condensation.

Today the plant output is approximately 4 tons per week, but possibly as much as 10 tons per week were produced at one time. The original equipment is used almost exclusively because there is still no better way of doing the same job and no better materials available. A plant installed for similar purposes today will vary little in design from that at Howards.

TOWER BRIDGE

Probably only Big Ben and Eros rival Tower Bridge as the London logo. Interestingly enough, none of them has laid claim to Londoners' and visitors' hearts because of their antiquity, since all three are firmly nineteenth century.

The original design of Tower Bridge was by Horace Jones, the city architect, modified by John Wolfe Barry assisted by Isambard Kingdom Brunel; the machinery was by Armstrong Mitchell (now Vickers-Armstrong). The total cost of the bridge exceeded £1,000,000.

> Asked to build an epoch-making suspension bridge that shall be drawbridge as well, he builds—in the nineteenth century—something like a mediaeval castle of granite, makes its towers look like a cross between a pair of Baptist chapels and Rhineland fortresses, spreads it massively across the sky and water, and, at the peak point of London's power and modernity, he creates a bridge suitable for King Arthur, the Black Prince, the archers of Agincourt, and operators of the culverin; in order, one supposes, to disguise from himself the fact that he has really built a masterpiece of engineering.[24]

Tower Bridge is indeed all these things. The original machinery, part of which can be seen in the photograph, is still in use and has never failed since the Prince of Wales (later Edward VII) performed the opening ceremony in June 1894. Hydraulic power for the bridge is provided by two 360 ihp tandem cross-compound steam pumping engines with a reserve engine of 250 ihp pumping into six hydraulic storage accumulators, each weighing approximately 100 tons. This storage capacity allows the bridge to be opened immediately when needed, and its weight produces a pressure in the hydraulic mains of 750 lb per sq. in. Over 1,000 tons of bascule can be raised in a minute and a half.

Each bascule leaf rotates on a shaft of 21 inches diameter which is carried on roller bearings, the visible portion being balanced by a counterpoise member. On each of these are mounted two geared quadrants which engage with pinions driven by the hydraulic engines. The two bascule leaves are held together at the centre by four hydraulically-operated locking bolts which can easily be seen from either footway. As a further safety precaution, pawls fall into place underneath the counterpoise when the bridge is in the lowered position.

A pedestrian way, 140 ft above the high-water mark, originally with public access, was closed, it was said, because it was an open invitation to suicides.

One of the lesser-known aspects of Tower Bridge, even to Londoners, is that a statutory order requires a tug always to be standing by to help any ship which might foul the piers of the bridge and to give any other assistance required. Surprisingly enough, the tug is used on average twice a day.

SMITHFIELD MARKET

With the growth of large towns, factory production and intensified commercial activity, the nature of the agricultural and retail markets underwent great changes. Contact between the growing areas of urban consumers and the rural producers became more difficult owing to the inability of the latter to supply the vastly expanded needs of the towns. It became necessary to draw upon suppliers from wider geographical areas. This created a demand for storage facilities and called into being terminal agricultural warehouses and markets. At the same time intermediaries increased and the character of the market changed from one where the consumer was the main purchaser to one in which the intermediaries were the customers.[25] Thus the central markets fulfilled, and continue to fulfil, a vital economic and physical function.

Typical of the London markets is Smithfield, which stands on the site of the 'Metropolitan Meat and Poultry Market', before that an open space of undefined extent where events such as Bartholomew's Fair were held. As early as 1150 it was used as a market for the sale of horses and cattle. In 1614 it was for the first time paved, drained and railed in, and extended over three acres. In 1852 the Corporation obtained an Act of Parliament for the removal of the 'live market' to Copenhagen Fields, Islington. The first two sections of the present Smithfield Market were opened in 1868 and additional sections were added as business expanded in 1875, 1889, 1898 and 1899.

The present building, with the air of both a railway station and a pier, is described as 'weakly Italianate'. It was designed by Horace Jones (who was also responsible for Billingsgate Market). Its main feature is unquestionably the covered roadway which divides it into two equal parts. This roadway unites the design, and supplies just that feature of interest needed to mark the centre of the building, breaking the monotony of the long north and south fronts. The roadway is 50 ft wide between the double piers which carry a richly moulded elliptical arch and pediment of cast iron. The sides of the roadway are shut off from the market by an elaborate screen of open ironwork, 14 ft high, and at its intersections with the central avenue, which runs east and west, the market is closed by gates of ornamental ironwork.

The gateways are 27 ft high (opening) and 19 ft wide and weigh 15 tons; the dimensions are 25 ft by 19 ft.

SPITALFIELDS SILK WEAVERS' HOUSES

Silk was first produced in England on any notable scale after the immigration about 1585 of a large body of skilled Flemish weavers who fled from the Low Countries during the conflict with Spain then devastating their land. One hundred years later the revocation of the Edict of Nantes caused numbers of skilled artisan silk weavers to emigrate from France to England. The bulk of the French Protestant weavers settled at Spitalfields, an incorporation of silk workers having been formed there in 1629.

Accommodation was provided for the silk weavers and their looms in an incredibly short time. The open ground outside the City wall at Bishopsgate was soon covered with a network of streets and alleys comprising houses specially built to meet the needs of weavers, embroiderers, silk dyers, throwsters and other craftsmen. Fleur de Lys Street, Blossom Street, Flower Street, Rose Alley are some of the original street names which still survive in the quarter where the weavers and their families first made their homes.[26]

Thrown silks were imported from the Continent until, after an early instance of industrial espionage by John Lombe of Derby who penetrated the Italian mills and made sketches of the machinery, local supplies could be produced.

The fame of Spitalfields silk attracted weavers into the area from all over the country. Well over 15,000 looms were in use in the last quarter of the eighteenth century, as the industry moved to the heights of its prosperity. Women always figured largely in silk weaving, and at this time it was difficult to find enough of them; so children were set to wind and quill while still in their infancy. This absorption of the entire family in periods of brisk trade led to the curious expedient of the Children's Market at Bethnal Green, where in an open space, from 6 a.m. to 8 a.m. every Monday and Tuesday, from 50 to 300 children from seven years of age presented themselves to be hired by the weavers.

During this period many of the elegant houses in the Spitalfields area were built. Number 14 Fournier Street, by common agreement the finest house in the street, was occupied commercially as early as 1743. Silk waste was found to have been packed between the floor joists to deaden the sound of looms in the garret.

The weavers' houses are distinguished by the attic workshops with a row of sash or casement windows along the front of the roof above the cornice. The top front room, the longest in the house, was used as a weaving shed. Instead of separate windows, as in the lower parts of the house, the whole front consists of

window with the minimum amount of brick or woodwork.

The prosperity of the industry was shortlived and by the end of the first quarter of the nineteenth century the condition of the silk weavers was desperate. Nevertheless in 1831 there were still 17,000 looms at work in east London, and a population of 100,000 in Spitalfields, Mile End, New Town and Bethnal Green, one-half of whom lived entirely from the manufacture of silk, the remainder being dependent to a lesser degree.

The commercial treaty with France in 1860 which allowed imports of cheap, foreign silks was the death blow to the industry. By the end of the century only a few of the most skilled weavers and some firms organizing their work in larger units survived. The fine nineteenth-century houses deteriorated and the area declined into infamy. Many of the weavers' homes were turned into cheap lodging-houses, the lamentable condition of which was the subject of much public and parliamentary comment. The worst slums of the district achieved an additional notoriety during the reign of terror of 'Jack the Ripper', for it was from this area his victims came.

Although many of the buildings in and around Fournier Street have been changed without feeling or consideration, the essential nature of their original purpose remains apparent in their garret workrooms.

FAIRGROUND MUSIC PUNCH IN CLERKENWELL

Fairground organs are now collectors' pieces. A late nineteenth- or early twentieth-century organ, which originally cost about £400, lovingly restored now fetches ten times that sum.

The organs work on the player piano (or pianola) principle. Perforated cardboard books in concertina form are drawn through a simple sensing mechanism, the valves of the organ and other instruments being actuated by the air released through the perforations. The books are made in 46- to 98-line widths. In the 46-line book there are eight base and ten vamping notes and the rest is melody. The large books have base, vamp, melody, counter-melody and percussion lines, since most organs include a range of percussion instruments, such as drums of various types and cymbals.

The first stage in the manufacture of the music books is the folding and glueing of the cardboard, back to back, to form the concertina strip, anything up to 100 yd long. This plays for 20 to 25 minutes. The music for transcription is first cut as a stencil which is then used to mark the books for the punch operator. The folded book is fed into a simple treadle-operated punching machine, the positioning of the music being controlled by a ratchet. Cutters from 5 mm to 14 mm are used laterally along each line, the whole length of the book. For holes longer than 14 mm, multiple cuts are made. At the end of the book, the operator moves the ratchet backward one notch and then proceeds to punch the next line. The bottom line, which is constantly handled by the operator in positioning the cardboard, is punched last to prevent damage to the holes.

The punching machine in the photograph, like most of the organs, is French and of unknown date but believed to be late nineteenth century. No new organs are being produced, although reconditioned ones cannibalized from old organs are still occasionally made. There are about sixty fairground organs still in use but most of the demand today is from collectors. Chiappi is now the only firm in Britain capable of repairing and servicing the organs, and supplying them with the perforated music. It seems that when the owner of this firm retires, a minor industry will cease to exist; there is no one to succeed him and his small band of elderly employees.

THE MINT STABLES AT PADDINGTON

It is easy to forget that the horse remained an important and integral part of railway operations until well after World War Two. For most of railway history the first and last stage of every journey for freight consignments was horse-drawn; and the same is true, over a shorter span of railway history, for passenger traffic. As a result a not inconsiderable number of horses had to be housed at the main-line termini.

Tucked away behind Paddington Station, to the east in Winsland Street, is what appears to be a prototype multi-storey garage. This building, however, was used to stable horses, not motor vehicles. Three floors with open galleries were connected by sloping ramps, just as in modern multi-storey garages. It is said that at the end of the day the many horses working at Paddington Station would find their own way back to the stables, mount the ramp and turn off at the correct gallery to their own stables—something cars cannot yet achieve!

The Mint Stables were constructed in 1878. The name comes from a house on the site which in turn is said to have succeeded a royal mint. The stables were constructed to hold approximately 600 horses; the basement held 50, the ground floor 260, the first floor 228, and the second floor 66.

The original structure of the stables remains largely unaltered, although considerable rebuilding took place in 1922 when the brickwork was resurfaced, and later the conversion of the building into offices involved the glazing of the open galleries. Much of the original cobbles and brickwork remains, as well as part of the balustrades and ramps into which wooden treads were once let to provide a grip for the horses' hooves.

LAUNCHING SITE OF THE *GREAT EASTERN*, ISLE OF DOGS

Perhaps the most ambitious failure in the whole history of naval architecture was the premature leviathan, conceived and built forty years in advance of relevant practical experience and the development of suitable materials. Designed by Isambard Kingdom Brunel, the *Great Eastern* (originally named the *Leviathan*) was to be five or six times the size of any vessel then in use and was intended for the Indian and Australian trade routes. It was believed the *Great Eastern* would maintain a speed of 15 knots with less power per ton than ordinary vessels required at 10 knots.[27]

The construction of the ship and her launching posed so many problems that their solution carried British engineering across several thresholds. The engines designed to turn the 58 ft diameter paddle wheels and 24 ft screw were said at that time to be powerful enough to drive all the cotton mills in Manchester. The bunker space was large enough to enable the vessel to steam nearly round the world without refuelling.

Of the constructional techniques and engineering novelties embodied in this great ship, three call for special mention. The first was the use of an experimental tank by William Froude in which the problems of stability and resistance could be studied. The second was the steam-operated steering gear designed by J. M. Gray; probably the first successful application of the hydraulic-servo or follow-up mechanism. The third was the major problem of actually launching the giant sideways.

It was the launching which provided the greatest drama of the vessel's eventful life which included a boiler explosion on the ship's trials, loss of the steering gear and paddles in a mid-Atlantic storm and an 85-ft hole torn in the outer skin by an uncharted reef at the entrance to Long Island Sound.[28]

After a career dotted with mishap and misfortune, and with the only commercial success related to cable laying rather than cargo and passenger carrying, the *Great Eastern*, after a period as a show-boat, was broken up in 1888.

Built at the Napier shipyard on the Isle of Dogs by John Scott Russell, at the time of the launch the *Great Eastern* weighed 12,000 tons and was 693 ft long and 118 ft wide. The ship rested in two cradles 80 ft square which were to slide on inclines 80 ft wide and 200 ft long set at a gradient of 1 in 14.

Russell's dubious financial stratagems ended in bankruptcy in 1856 after construction had begun. The mortgagees of his property allowed the Great

Eastern Company occupancy of the yard and use of the plant until 12 August 1857, giving Brunel fourteen months to move the vessel into the Thames. It is said that at this time well over half the work still remained to be done. By January 1857 the contract for the launching ways and cradles was let, but as the August deadline could not be achieved an extension was negotiated until 5 October 1857, the company having to agree to a rental of £2,500, described as exorbitant. The agreement had again to be extended to 3 November.

The launch presented the greatest challenge of Brunel's career. Hampered as he was by sightseers and an inadequate communication system, the great vessel stuck, after moving a few feet, and in so doing killed one man and injured others manning a winch. The launch was abandoned until 19 November but no further progress was made then. On 28 November a further 14 ft were achieved. Brunel decided to depend exclusively on hydraulic power, and further attempts were made on 30 November and 2 December. After this any hope of a December launch passed.

It was at this point Brunel called on the Tangye brothers for their new hydraulic presses which were delivered to him by the end of the year. The performance of these presses at Millwall was such that it laid the foundation of a great business and it was Tangyes' boast that 'we launched the *Great Eastern* and the *Great Eastern* launched us'.

During the whole of this period Brunel and the Great Eastern Company were under constant and blackmailing pressure from the mortgagees, and a barrage of criticism from the press.[29]

On 5 January 1858, a further attempt was made: on 10 January the ship was partially waterborne. Operations were suspended until the high tides of the 19th passed, which might have floated her prematurely. Finally, on 31 January 1858 the ship was afloat. The victory had been purchased at a terrible price. The company was ruined and Brunel's health broken.

A sign now clearly marks the site and a few timbers exposed at low tide are the last relics of an epic struggle against the perversity of machines and the mendacity of men.

BREWERY IN CHISWELL STREET

Breweries have provided more evidence of their history, and for a longer period of time, than the majority of industrial activities. The sense of tradition and continuity is perhaps high, or the original buildings and equipment were of such good design, or so well anticipated changing needs, that much has survived; for economic as well as historical or even sentimental reasons, London abounds with breweries of outstanding interest. Foremost is the Whitbread brewery in Chiswell Street, the only one within the boundaries of the City of London.

In 1750 Samuel Whitbread bought the King's Head brewery which was on part of the present site, and over the years the site and buildings were extended. Part of the original acquisition was a handsome early eighteenth-century house which still exists.

Some of the greatest names in engineering were associated with building and equipping the brewery; James Watt, John Rennie and John Smeaton were among them. Smeaton designed six underground storage cisterns. Rennie superintended the erection of machinery when Whitbread introduced steam power in 1775. The steam engine, designed by Boulton & Watt, was one of the wonders of London: it is now in the Museum of Technology in Sydney, Australia.

Like many old breweries, the one in Chiswell Street has impressive interiors using timber constructions. Large quantities of malt had to be stored in advance of brewing; the porter, once brewed, matured for anything up to nine months. The Porter Tun Room, originally the 'Great Storehouse' and 162 ft 6 in long by 65 ft wide, is one of the few of these storerooms to survive. It was completed in 1784 and has a spectacular open timber roof: its unsupported span is exceeded only by one in Westminster Hall. The care with which the builders chose their timbers for the lofty roof is clearly shown by the way it survived the effects of bombs and anti-aircraft shrapnel during World War Two.

SEALING-WAX FACTORY IN BERMONDSEY

The practice of authenticating important state documents by affixing a seal to them which was emblematic of the governing power dates back to remote antiquity. Gems and cylinder seals were used extensively until the fall of the Roman Empire but the practice by the Popes of using lead or gold *bullae* continued. At one time seals were as extensively used by private individuals as by state and church dignitaries and other officials.

Sealing-wax was developed in mediaeval times almost solely for the purpose of attaching the impression of official seals to documents. Its composition used to be a mixture of Venice turpentine, bees'-wax and colouring matter, usually vermilion. Today sealing-wax generally consists of a rosin base, baryta, paraffin-wax and pigments. The method of manufacture has changed very little, however.

The materials are melted together in a large cast-iron melting bowl and periodically stirred. The correct moment for pouring is judged rather than measured. The poured wax hardens rapidly in the moulds and after fettling the sticks are passed quickly through a small furnace which expands and bursts any airholes. A second passage through the furnace glazes the wax to its finished stage.

The production machinery is simplicity itself. The large cast-iron grinding machine in the foreground of the photograph, taken at the Cooper, Dennison & Walkden factory, is believed to be over 200 years old and is still at work. There is every likelihood that the equipment was in use when Richard Walkden conducted his business from a house *on* London Bridge. The cast-iron melting bowls, also over 200 years old, would today cost more than £250 each to replace. The polishing furnace consisting of enclosed gas jets has a railed track running through it on which trolleys, carrying the unfinished wax sticks, are placed. In the photograph these are being arranged on the trolley prior to passing through the furnace on the extreme left of the picture. Other production equipment includes wooden 'bats' for handling and shaping, and metal and wooden moulds.

Sealing-wax is principally used today, of course, for sealing postal parcels, legal documents, bottles, money packets and postage-stamp rolls. The red wax, which has been used over the centuries, still dominates demand but wide ranges of other colours are now available, largely to meet requirements of export markets.

PLATE EDGE-PLANER, ISLE OF DOGS

The rapid acceptance of steam power in the nineteenth century, with its sharp stimulus to the development of new products, demanded better methods of manufacture and new machinery. Needless to say, the manufacture of boilers for the steam raising was a considerable industry, which in turn created demands for special metal-working machinery. One such piece of equipment was the plate edge-planer.

Plate edge-planers were used to machine a chamfer, or slanting edge, on to boiler plates. The plates were then passed through rollers, rather in the manner of the cold rolling machine illustrated earlier in the book. Only three rollers were used, however; one of these was above the plate and two below. The metal passing through gradually took up a cylindrical shape. The joint was then riveted together. The edges which now met required caulking to make the boiler steam-tight and this operation was considerably assisted by the chamfered edge of the plate. This edge was hammered with a chisel to integrate it and to close the gap.

The plate edge-planer at John Fraser & Sons Ltd has a bed 20 ft long with a cast-iron back fitted with twenty screw clamps. The plate is inserted under the back and clamped down. The tool rest travels along the bed driven by a worm gear. Originally it only cut in one direction, but in 1922 it was modified so that the tool rest could be turned over and another tool brought in line for the return journey. The worm was originally driven from a counter-shaft but when the modification was made a DC motor was fitted. The speed is governed by the drum-type controller seen in the photograph.

The machine was used in making the original dry back boilers for the Willesden and Bankside power stations. It is now only operated occasionally, as most boilers and tanks made at Frasers have welded seams. The plate edge-planer was manufactured in 1888 by Smith, Beacock & Tannet of Leeds.

WOODEN WINCH IN ST PAUL'S CATHEDRAL

Pieces of early construction equipment are among the rarer items of industrial equipment to be found in London. A less appropriate site than St Paul's Cathedral is unlikely to be encountered; yet, 320 ft above London, higher indeed than the modern buildings which surround the Cathedral, there remains on site a wooden winch.

This winch stands above the Golden Gallery and immediately beneath the Ball. Neither its date nor its purpose are positively known, but it may have been installed to haul up the external railings which surround the Golden Gallery. These railings can be identified as of 1832 manufacture, so that if the supposition is correct the winch is either of that date or older. If, however, the winch was used to haul up the internal fittings and other materials, it seems likely its date is even earlier: the internal fittings, to judge from their condition and environmental factors, are older than the external ones.

Another mystery is why the winch should have been left in position at all once its work was finished. Whatever the reason, it remains and is easily accessible to anyone who has the energy to climb the 627 stairs.

The metal work of the winch beam bears the just visible legend 'James Walker, 26 Harp Alley, Fleet Market, London'. The wooden drums are still in excellent condition and its gearing in perfect order. An isometric projection of the Cathedral, by Brook Greaves, dated 1923, in the Victoria & Albert Museum, clearly shows the position of the winch in relation to the gallery.

Also in St Paul's Cathedral, in the north-west bell tower, not generally accessible to the public, is a wooden capstan of unknown but considerable age. In its present position, where it is mounted vertically, there would not have been enough room to turn it, so it must be in the bell tower as a relic. A search of the records of the Cathedral throws no light on its maker, purpose or date.

THE WHITECHAPEL BELL FOUNDRY

Bells have been made at Whitechapel since the early part of Queen Elizabeth I's reign. A list of them would fill a volume but perhaps the most famous are Big Ben, Big Tom, the Liberty Bell, Bow Bells and St Clement Danes' Bell.

The workshop at the bell foundry, dating back almost 400 years, is probably the oldest in the country which is still in daily use. Cannon and all types of other brass foundry-work were also cast there, including, it is claimed, cannons used against the Armada.

The photograph shows a hand-lathe made by 'Knight of Foster Lane' which is still in use. Originally it was driven by a hand-operated fly-wheel but has now been modified and uses an electric motor. The bed and blocks forming the head-stock and tailstock are solid mahogany, and all the bolts are hand made. The excellence of the original design can be judged by the fact that its owners have had two other lathes made to exactly the same design.

The lathe is used in the manufacture of hand-bells. The rough castings are turned and polished on it, and during this process the tuning is carried out.

The foundry possesses many other early examples of industrial activity but of particular interest is a crane, dating from around 1738, which is fixed to the wall above the yard entrance. This is operated by a hand winch and is still used to lift loads up to $1\frac{1}{2}$ tons.

PUMPING STATION AT KEW BRIDGE

Most large towns assumed responsibility for their own water supplies in the second half of the nineteenth century, although London water, the quality of which had frequently been censured by medical authorities, remained in the control of private companies until the establishment of the Metropolitan Water Board in 1904.

Kew Bridge pumping station was built by the Grand Junction Water Works Company incorporated in 1811 to supply Paddington and the adjacent parishes. The works were established near what is now Paddington Station and water was originally drawn from the Grand Junction Canal. The quality of this water proved inferior to that of the Thames, and the company opened a new works at Chelsea where, in 1820, two beam engines and pumps by Boulton, Watt & Company were erected.

The Chelsea supply was in turn condemned and a fresh intake was arranged at Kew Bridge. In 1852 the Metropolitan Water Act forced the companies drawing water from the Thames to operate from above Teddington Lock. The Kew Bridge works were retained, however, as a filtration and pumping station and eventually came into the possession of the Metropolitan Water Board.

The dismantled engines from the Chelsea works were re-erected in the impressive engine house which still stands at Kew. One of the original engines remains, and other interesting steam pumping engines by Henry Maudslay, Andrew Vivian and the Harveys of Hayle were either erected later to serve at Kew, or have since been brought there from other stations for preservation. None of them has pumped into supply since 1944.

Kew Bridge pumping station now contains five Cornish engines, the earliest of which is a 'West' beam engine by Boulton & Watt which began work in 1820 at Chelsea and was re-erected at Kew Bridge in 1839/40. It was converted to the Cornish principle in 1846. A Maudslay beam engine of 1838, which was converted to the Cornish principle at the same time as the Boulton & Watt engines, is also installed at Kew, as well as 70-, 90- and 100-in engines. This last, a Cornish beam engine by Harvey & Company of Hayle, Cornwall, is probably the largest single-cylinder Cornish engine still in existence: the photograph shows its beam.

The Kew Bridge works still act as a re-pumping station for filtered water from Hampton. The machinery consists of six electrically-driven and four oil-driven centrifugal pumps.

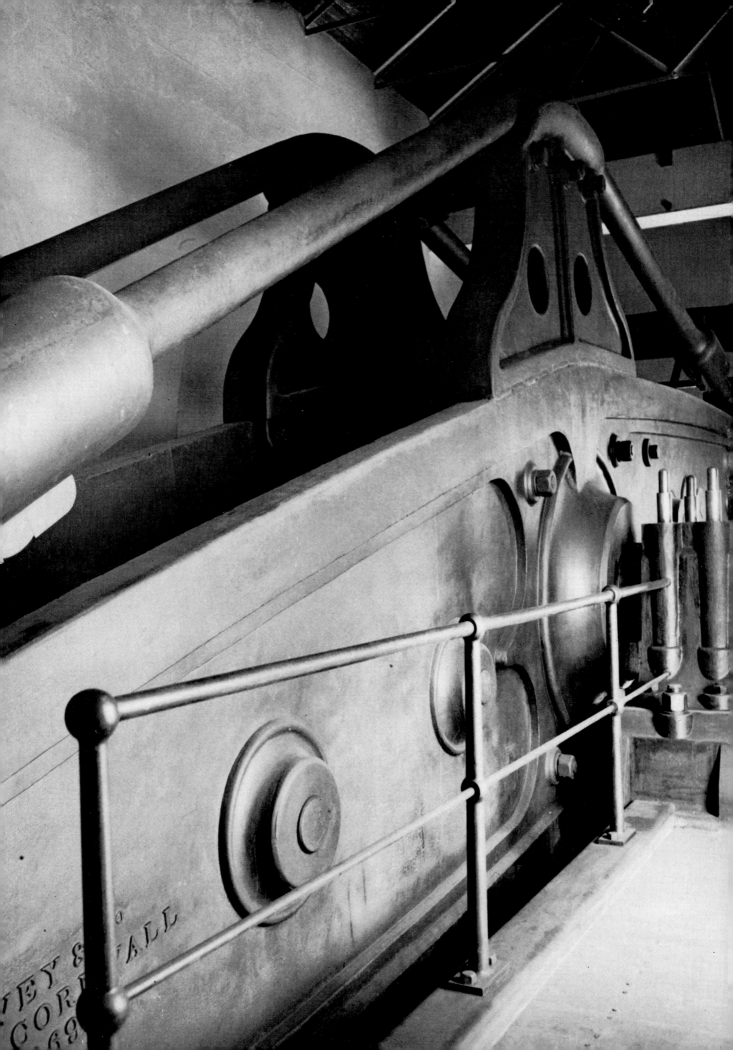

SNUFF MILLS AT MORDEN

Along with windmills, water mills are the first examples of buildings evolved for the purpose of housing machinery; they mark the beginning of industry as separate non-domestic activity.

As recently as forty years ago, over thirty water mills bestraddled the River Wandle between Croydon and Wandsworth. These included tobacco, copper, oil, leather, flour, parchment and paper mills. At Morden Hall, within a stone's throw of the Underground, two water mills still exist which were originally used for grinding snuff. The age of the older mill, standing on the east bank adjacent to Morden Cottage, is not known exactly but certainly it is not later than eighteenth century; the mill on the western bank is much more recent, dating from about 1860.

The two large cast-iron wheels are original but the paddles and floats are modern replacements. The grinding mechanism in the earlier mill consisted of a Yorkshire granite ring set in the floor with two large granite mill stones which rolled around it, fixed to a centre pivot. The granite ring in the floor still exists (although it can no longer be seen as it is covered with a cement screed); the mill stones lie outside.

The later mill was operated by a series of elm mortars with cast-iron pestles powered by the water wheel. The machinery was sold for scrap in 1939 except for the mill wheels and one large cast-iron wheel which is stored in an adjacent shed. This wheel was originally fitted horizontally in the upper floor and worked the pestles.

The raw material for the mills consisted of tobacco refuse, including leaves and stalks not suitable for smoking—no doubt drawn, in part, from other mills on the Wandle. It was processed in kilns outside the mills, and taken back to the mill for grinding. The pulverized material was sifted by 'dressers' and mixed.

For a while business at the mills was so brisk that they were working twenty-four hours a day, seven days a week, on a shift system. However, changing tastes spelt the demise of snuff and they finally closed down shortly after World War One.

Both mill buildings are in the care of the National Trust, but it is planned to remove one of the water wheels in the near future to improve the flow of the river. It is small consolation that the remaining wheel will, at the same time, be put into good repair.

EAST INDIA COMPANY WAREHOUSES, BISHOPSGATE

'. . . the towering warehouses of the East India Company (now Port of London Authority), six-storeyed, with a minimum of classical stone detail below, bare red brick above. They were begun in 1782 and cover about five acres.' So comments Pevsner,[30] and the dry description hides history, innovation and romance.

The warehouses were built by the East India Company after Clive's victories when the growth of business outstripped available accommodation. At the end of the eighteenth century, the company had warehouses on twelve sites in the City, and riverside depots at Billingsgate and Ratcliffe. Each warehouse was intended for a single class of goods.

Construction of the new warehouses began in 1793, the company making separate agreements with master men in nine trades, each to execute part of the work. No demarcation disputes seem to have occurred, the construction being carried through in five stages and completed in 1801, at a cost of £241,632. Richard Jupp, the supervisor, died in 1799; he was succeeded by Henry Holland, a pioneer in the construction of fireproof buildings. Holland introduced his system of arches built with hollow clay pots into the landings of the staircases, which can clearly be seen in the photograph.

For nearly a century from the opening of the first warehouse, all goods were handled manually. In 1868 a small hoist was installed, for moving tea; it was worked by steam raised in a gas-fired boiler which, to satisfy the requirements of the Fire Offices, was placed on the roof. Hydraulic power was introduced in 1888 although today it is supplemented by electric hoists.

The warehouses have been used to store piece goods, raw silk for the nearby Spitalfields weavers, tea, ostrich feathers, isinglass and opium. Over 600 tons of cigars still pass through the bond each year. By far the most important commodities found today are Oriental carpets and European wines.

CLOCK GEARWHEEL-CUTTING MACHINE IN CLERKENWELL

Thwaites & Reed, founded in 1740 by Aynsworth Thwaites, are the oldest established clockmakers in the United Kingdom, with complete records, housed in the Guildhall Library, going back to that date. The company have exported clocks to almost every country in the world, and specialize in the production of public and special clocks. They are also concerned with the restoration and winding of clocks all over the country. Much of their machinery was installed in the middle of the last century and because of its simplicity and accuracy is still in use.

One item of particular interest is a gearwheel-cutting machine made by Thwaites & Reed for their own use over 100 years ago. Made of cast-iron and similar in shape to a treadle sewing machine, it is 4 ft long with a 3 ft long 'bed'. It was originally operated by treadle and later a gas engine, but is now driven by an overhead belt connected to an electric motor.

Gear wheels of varying sizes up to 2 ft 10 in can be made on the machine. The wheel to be cut is trued into position and clamped down firmly on the right side of the 'bed'. The cutter is attached to an upright which can be moved to and fro along the 'bed' by turning the large wheel on the left. The actual positioning is governed by the size of the gearwheel to be cut. A brass divided plate, lying horizontally under the 'bed' and attached to the turntable carrying the gearwheel, has thirty-two varying-sized rings of notches. A stop linked by a metal arm to the cutter is pushed by hand into the selected notches on the divided plate until a full circle has been completed. By depressing a handle on the upright, the cutter comes down on to the gearwheel and makes a toothlike incision. This process continues until the set number of 'teeth' have been cut into the wheel.

Many public clocks had their gearwheels manufactured on this machine, among the more famous being that of the restored church of St Mary-le-Bow (Bow Bells), the clock in the very ancient, badly bombed All Hallows-by-the-Tower church, and the new but already well-known clock at Fortnum & Mason.

THE REGENTS PARK DIORAMA

The Panorama and Diorama are part of the pre-history of the cinema. The Panorama is usually attributed to the painter Robert Barker, who first exhibited the fully developed entertainment in Leicester Square in 1792. This consisted of an enormous canvas attached to the inside of a rotunda revolving slowly round the spectators seated in the centre—perhaps a forerunner of the short-lived 'Circlorama' recently located at Piccadilly Circus. The machinery of the Panorama resembled a post mill. Placed in semi-darkness, the audience gazed across a gulf of about 12 ft at a continuous moving picture lit from above. The invention was shown in Paris where it achieved an immediate success and began to multiply in all the capital cities of Europe and America.[31] The Panorama was, however, soon surpassed as a public attraction by the Diorama.

> This delightful exhibition is a display of architectural and landscape scenery, painted in solid, and in transparency, arranged and lighted in a peculiar mode, so as to exhibit changes of light and shade, and a variety of natural phenomena in a really wonderful manner. The pictures are lighted from behind by large windows as big as pictures, and by sky-lights over and in front of them; and by the aid of opaque and transparent screens and curtains of various colours and degrees of transparency, the various effects of light, shade and gradations of colour are produced. These pictures are viewed from a very elegant circular theatre, with pit, boxes and passages, through an opening, decorated by a proscenium. While the opening in the theatre is before one picture, the whole body of the audience part is slowly moved round by some admirable machinery below and the spectators, seats, attendants and all, are moved imperceptibly round, from the Mary Chapel of Canterbury Cathedral to Lake Lausanne, or from the city of Rouen in France to the interior of Rosslyn Chapel in Scotland.[32]

A hand ratchet operated cords which ran over a pulley at the top of the building down to a bar on a fulcrum. Movement of this bar altered the colouring and shading of the pictures.

The revolving floor was supported on strong timber framework consisting of a central shaft with twelve timber arms radiating from it jointed by pentagonal cross pieces at the perimeter. These cross pieces carried the bearings of the twelve iron shafts which in turn were the axis to twelve cast-iron rollers. The rollers ran on a circular metal track bolted to the masonry. The main shaft was bolted to a brass step-piece.

The movement was not in fact a full 360° circle but covered some 73° in a slow oscillation, exhibiting pictures alternately. The whole mechanism was moved by a winch connected by gearing to the central shaft. The winch had a flywheel to permit smooth operation.

Diorama buildings were once as numerous in the major cities of the world as cinemas are today, but only one is now known to exist. This is the one shown in the photograph and is at Regent's Park. The façade was designed by John Nash and the rotunda and picture emplacements by J. G. Pugin and James Morgan.

REMAINS OF THE CROYDON ATMOSPHERIC RAILWAY

The atmospheric system of motive power, patented by the Samuda Brothers, was not perhaps passed in sheer ingenuity until the development of the linear accelerator. In practice, and despite the influential support of I. K. Brunel, it was a disastrous failure, defeated largely by the inadequacies of the materials available at the time and the high initial cost of the fixed equipment. The idea was to remove the power source from the train and to construct fixed power stations along the track at intervals. This principle had already been used extensively for drawing trains up steep inclines by rope haulage, but the Clegg and Samuda patents used the pressure of the atmosphere to propel the train.

The London & Croydon Railway Company decided to use the atmospheric system of traction for a separate local line free from main-line interference. William Cubitt, the engineer to the Croydon company, studied the results obtained with atmospheric traction in Ireland and recommended the addition to the London and Croydon sections of the route of a single atmospheric line for Croydon local traffic. The line was eventually built between Dartmouth Arms (Forest Hill) and Croydon (now West Croydon), and extended and operated for a few months to New Cross.

Trial runs, with the passengers travelling free of charge, began in the autumn of 1845. Regular running began in January 1847 with trains from London Bridge discarding their locomotives at Forest Hill and then proceeding behind the piston carriage. By May 1846, after some considerable re-building of equipment and pipes, the line was carrying a regular hourly service from London Bridge, changing over as before at Forest Hill, with four additional semi-fast trains and corresponding up workings. The fastest trains covered the five miles in seven minutes.[33]

Traction was achieved by a continuous 15 in diameter iron pipe between the rails with a slot along the top which was enclosed by a well-greased leather valve stiffened with iron, made up in 8-in sections. Into this pipe went a piston connected by an arm to the train. Stationary engines at intervals along the line exhausted the air in the tube ahead of the piston, so that the atmospheric pressure behind the piston drove the train along. Behind the piston arm, the valve was re-sealed by a system of rollers combined with a re-greasing device—a sort of flat iron heated by charcoal which melted the grease composition so that it ran into interstices and made the valve airtight after the device had passed over it.

As a means of transmitting power the system was probably more efficient

than any other then available. It did not lend itself to the operation of switching the train from one line to another and it was impossible to work through cross-overs. At Forest Hill the trains crossed the steam lines by previously acquired momentum, both staff and passengers hoping that the carriages would not stop before they had their piston safely into the next section of pipe. But even in 1844 railway engineers were mainly pre-occupied with getting the trains from one station to another.[34]

The operating procedure was to telegraph the first engine house down the line where the engine would start. When it had obtained a vacuum of 16 in or more ahead of the piston, the train moved off. Seventy mph were clocked on trial, and an average of 40 mph was achieved start-to-stop, with a six-coach train full of passengers. However, as with the other atmospheric lines (Dublin-Kingstown and the South Devon Railway), mechanical failure occurred constantly. Apart from difficulties with the stationary engines and pumps, the valve-sealing method was inadequate, particularly in hot weather when the grease would not set.

After less than two years, the last atmospheric train ran on the Croydon line and the equipment was sold. The Forest Hill engine house remained until struck by a flying bomb in 1944. The Croydon engine house, in the photograph, was bought for £250 by the Croydon Local Board of Health for a pumping station for the main water supply. It was dismantled and re-erected on the present site in 1851.[35]

LINOLEUM PRESSES AT STAINES

Linoleum has a surprisingly long history. The first patent, dating back as far as 1636, for 'painting with oyle cullers upon woollen cloth' being followed by the use of various oils and resins. In 1751 India-rubber or gum lastic was incorporated. A factory set up in Knightsbridge in 1754 manufactured floor cloth by applying to canvas a mixture of rosin, pitch, Spanish brown, bees'-wax and linseed oil in a melted state and rolling it by pressure.

It was not, however, until 1860 that 'linoleum' proper appeared, the term being coined by Frederick Walton who took out a patent. Walton invented a process of oxidizing linseed oil to produce a cheap rubber-like substitute. The solidified oil was then ground between rollers and heated in a steam-jacketed pan, together with rosin and kauri gum. The resulting mass, a dark homogeneous thick liquid, when cooled in thin layers became a sticky rubber-like material. By mixing with cork dust, wood flour, whiting and pigments, 'linoleum' material was produced. The mixture was ground by passing through a series of rollers and fed continuously into a 'scratcher', a machine consisting of two rollers, one steam heated and the other cold, to which the material adhered, forming a thick layer. All types of linoleum passed through these stages but from hereon the method of manufacture differed, depending upon the type of finish required.

The Fielding & Platt 1,300-ton press in the photograph was one of a batch of twenty-eight manufactured between 1888 and 1906. Seventeen of the presses are still in productive use. Of the others, one at least has been adapted to a modern technology and is producing aircraft components, utilizing the latest rubber-mould technique.

A few of the original presses were supplied with a steel liner pressed into position and used as a main ram guide-sleeve, easily replaceable if necessary. The steel used in the columns was of an extremely ductile nature, characteristic of the steels of the day, and this combined with the absence of shock loading probably accounts for the long life of presses manufactured at this time. Moreover, because there was little knowledge of complex stressing such as is common today, greater margins of safety than necessary were incorporated.

THE KINGSWAY TRAM TUNNEL

When the last London tram finally ran into its depot on 5 July 1952, it brought to an end the use of a unique part of the London transport system, the Kingsway tram tunnel—the prototype of all the underpasses which have since been constructed in London to ease road congestion. It is fitting perhaps that the major part of the original tunnel has been converted into a two-lane motor underpass between Waterloo Bridge and Kingsway. But part of the old tunnel remains intact and unused, from its entrance at the junction of Theobalds Road and Southampton Row to the exit of the present underpass.

The idea of a shallow underground tramway to link the tramway systems of north and south London was first officially mooted in 1899. After investigations in New York and Boston, the London County Council obtained powers to construct a subway starting at Theobalds Road, following the line of the new street, now known as Kingsway, and passing underneath the Strand to emerge on Victoria Embankment.

Work on street and subway began simultaneously and the tramway as far south as Aldwych opened in 1906; the first tram ran over the completed route in 1908. The subway was five-eighths of a mile long and included several different forms of construction.

At the northern end, shown in the photograph and still much as it was when first built, an incline in the middle of the road 170 ft long and 20 ft wide, with a gradient of 1 in 10, led to twin tunnels of cast-iron of 14 ft 5 in diameter and 255 ft long; these carried the track under two pipe subways and a branch of the Fleet sewer beneath Holborn. The incline then rose in a reverse 1 in 10 gradient into Holborn station. From Holborn to Aldwych the distance was 1,880 ft and the tracks ran in a single 20-ft-wide tunnel of rectangular sections with a roof of steel troughing just below the level of the street. At Aldwych the tunnel turned westward and dipped in a 1 in 20 gradient to pass under the Strand. This section, 440 ft long, had brickwork arches instead of steel troughing. Under the Strand itself, the single tunnel reverted to twin cast-iron tubes similar to those under Holborn. These tubes curved and came to an end at the first brick piers of the viaduct leading to Waterloo Bridge (which consisted of sixteen arches carried on brick piers).

The final section involved underpinning 360 ft of this viaduct to permit openings being made to accommodate a 20-ft-wide single tunnel—a delicate

operation, since the failure of any of the piers would have resulted in the collapse of the whole street. To give access to the subway from Victoria Embankment, a portal was constructed next to the old Waterloo Bridge. The southern wing of the abutment, which incorporated a small stairway arch, was carefully dismantled and re-erected to allow for a 22 ft 6 in diameter archway.

The usefulness of the tram link was at first limited because it could not take double-decked cars, an idea originally rejected because of the steep gradient necessary to enable a subway with sufficient headroom to pass under the Fleet sewer. It was 1930 before the enlargement began, the subway re-opening in 1931. The extra headroom was achieved by raising the roof of the tunnel for a short section at the northern end and lowering the rail level elsewhere. North of Holborn the two cast-iron tubes and brick arches were replaced by a new steel roof on steel stanchions built into concrete side walls, forming one wide tunnel just below street level. The Fleet sewer was diverted into the Kingsway sewer.[36]

Between Holborn and the Strand the side walls of the single tunnel were underpinned and the tracks lowered. Under the Strand, where the tracks were again carried in twin tubes, the lower segments of the tubes were removed in short lengths and new concrete walls built to carry the upper segments temporarily supported on timber. While this work proceeded the stations at Holborn and Aldwych were modernized and enlarged new lighting installed.

The latest type double-deck tram cars were put into service through the enlarged subway which re-opened on 15 January 1931, with three services involving 5,000 journeys a week replacing the previous single service.

When the new Waterloo Bridge was built the extreme southern end of the subway was realigned to bring the Embankment portal immediately beneath the bridge. The original work and the later modifications cost in total almost £500,000.

The reconstructed subway, however, saw only twenty-one years of operation before its final closure and partial conversion to a motor underpass.

THE BRIXTON WINDMILL

Windmills, both because of their beauty and their pastoral-romantic associations, have attracted the attention of the preservationists possibly more than any other physical manifestation of manufacturing buildings and machinery. Probably only the railways and canals vie with windmills for the attention of the industrial archaeologist. The architectural form evolved by windmills is a splendid example of the challenge of function producing a style of architecture both elegant and robust.

The windmill at Brixton, erected about 1816, is of the tower type. The main structure is of 14-in-thick brickwork with a wooden boat-type cap which, at one time, revolved. It stands 49 ft high and is 22 ft 3 in about the base. Many of the beams used in its construction are reputed to be much older and are probably ships' timbers.

The mill had a working life of just over fifty years, after which new buildings in the area prevented the wind from reaching it in sufficient force to turn the sails. The flour-milling business was transferred to a water mill on the Wandle where, after a time, once again the power source failed; the water flow became insufficient to provide the required power. This gave the Brixton windmill a new lease of life as it was refitted and adapted to modern use by the addition of first a steam and then a gas engine.

The fight to preserve the mill has been a long one, ending in 1954 with the acquisition of the site by the London County Council by a compulsory purchase order. The Council then laid out the site as an open space and, although the mill house was demolished, the mill itself was restored and new sails, made by a Lincolnshire millwright, were fitted. The machinery has not been restored, however, and the sails are unlikely ever to move again.

THE WHARNCLIFFE VIADUCT

This early example of Brunel's constructive genius is named after the first Lord Wharncliffe for 'zealous and indefatigable services rendered to the Great Western Railway Company'. His coat of arms decorates the centre southern face of the viaduct which carries the Great Western Railway line over the River Brent. The Bristol end of the line was the concern of a separate committee, independent of the one which worked at the London end. As a result, a difference in emphasis on the importance of various types of structures can be noticed.[37] The Bristol end has an elegance which contrasts with the more functional approach of the London end, nowhere better typified than in the Wharncliffe Viaduct—which *The Official Illustrated Guide to the Great Western Railway 1860* notes as 'the largest piece of brickwork on the railway'.

Construction began in February 1836 and was completed by the summer of 1837. The viaduct is 900 ft long and consists of eight semi-elliptical arches, each with a span of 70 ft and a rise of 17 ft 6 in. The massive piers and abutments are in fact hollow, combining economy and strength with a considerable saving in weight. The piers were originally constructed with two square pillars with a base of 252 sq. ft and foundations going down to about 17 ft. The foundation's clay bed, however, caused the embankments to slip and by November 1837 the slipping was as much as $1\frac{1}{2}$ in per day. This was remedied by increasing the weight and spread of the terraces which had been formed on the north side as counterweights to the embankment.

The viaduct was originally 30 ft wide, a standard Brunel adopted for all embankments and viaducts. This allowed for a double line of broad-gauge rails (14 ft $0\frac{1}{2}$ in) with space between the up and down line of 6 ft (hence the 'six-foot way'), and space outside each line of 5 ft. In 1861 mixed gauge was introduced, and in 1874 the viaduct was widened by the construction of an additional pillar for each of the seven piers on the north side of the viaduct. The original 30 ft became 52 ft. May 1892 saw the end of the wide gauge and the need for a mixed-gauge track no longer existed. Both wide and mixed gauge thus passed into oblivion.

RAM BREWERY BEAM ENGINES, WANDSWORTH

Breweries have provided industrial archaeologists with some most rewarding finds. In London, Whitbreads in Chiswell Street, Trumans in Spitalfields, and Charringtons in Mile End are all of outstanding interest.

Still operating today and providing the main power source at Young's Ram Brewery in Wandsworth is an 1867 beam engine by Wentworth & Sons of Wandsworth, the low-pressure cylinder of which can be seen in the photograph. Even more remarkable and working 'like a sewing machine' is a second smaller engine used for standby power purposes and originally installed in 1835. The smaller engine was erected for 12 hp and converted to 16 hp in 1863.

Both engines are connected by belts to the central drive shaft which runs up through three floors of the brewery. They drive through gearing fitted with horn-beam (a very hard wood) teeth, shafts and dog clutches, and operate three three-throw vertical pumps and one two-throw pump, as well as driving additional shafting and pumps for the circulation of mash and beer.

The gearing on the central drive shaft is separated from the beam engines by a wall. Both engines have the usual A-shape frames, cast-iron beams with lattice-work eccentric rods and links suspended from the beams. The valve gears have vertical guides and swinging links, and the flywheels are of wrought iron.

The brewery is a treasure-house of items to interest the industrial archaeologist and historian. Milling machinery and large copper vessels, over 100 years old, are still in use. Regrettably, all the early records of the brewery were lost in a flood.

THE CAMDEN TOWN CATACOMBS

The importance of the horse in railway operations was pointed out earlier in the book in discussing the multi-storey Mint Stables at Paddington. There is little doubt that the economies of horse operations accounted largely for their persistence long into the era of the internal-combustion engine. A railway horse cost approximately £60; fodder about 9s 6d per week; the average life was five and a half years, during which time it worked about ten hours a day. Horses could pull loads of up to 30 cwt alone or 4 tons in pairs.

At the turn of the century, before motor vehicles became ubiquitous, the movement as well as the stabling of horses must certainly have been a major problem because of the large numbers involved. If the solution to stabling horses at Paddington was to build upwards, the answer at Camden was to go underground.

The origin of the extensive tunnels and vaults which honeycomb the area under Camden goods station is shrouded in mystery. In 1855 a contemporary writer notes that:

> Horses were used at Camden Station to move railway trucks and wagons into position. Because of the difficulty of finding stabling for such a number of horses close at hand, they were lodged in the underground vaults at Camden but whether this was the original purpose for these vaults cannot be ascertained.

At a later date the tunnels were certainly in use to allow horses to move to and from their quarters without having to cross the network of railway lines above. The tunnels also provided a connection between other stables in Gloucester Road, alongside the north bank of Regents Canal, and the goods depot on the other side of the main line. Just how many horses were at Camden is not known, but in the early years of this century there were over 1,200 based at Kings Cross a short distance away; the Great Eastern Railway had a similar number at Liverpool Street; and in 1909 the Great Western Railway had 600 horses at Paddington.

For a number of years the vaults were part of Gilbeys' bonded warehouses, barges unloading directly into them from Regents Canal. From behind rusted iron doors its sinister lap can still be heard.

Today the catacombs are used for storage and the dimly-lit tunnels are devoid of life other than the occasional railway worker. But old notices which can still be seen evoke their past. One reads: 'Horses passing through this tunnel must be led by the person in charge of them. Any person neglecting this rule will be discharged.'

OFFICES IN FULHAM ROAD

When Michelin, the French tyre firm, decided a new and suitably impressive base for their British operations was needed, designs were made at the Clermont Ferrand headquarters in France which produced a building in a flamboyant, architectural and decorative style. It stands in true early-twentieth-century splendour in an area increasingly dominated by the architecture of the mid-twentieth century and has been described as 'one of the least likely buildings in an unlikely city'. The architect appears to have been a M. Espinasse. More than that is not known.

The offices, opened in 1910, included every modern refinement of their time —mosaic floors, tiled walls and automatically opening doors. Outside and in, coloured tiles made by Gilardoni of Paris, tell the story of early motoring triumphs —Henri Farman driving his Panhard to victory in the 1902 Paris-to-Vienna race; Albert Guillame in a rakish Daracq; and Marcel Renault travelling at speed. In place of honour is that pioneer motorist, Edward VII and his son, later George V.

The building was originally dominated by a huge Bibendum—Michelin's well-known tyre-man symbol—which glowed out on to Fulham Road at night from the main upper-floor windows, lit by mercury vapour lamps. Another Bibendum appeared in a floor mosaic in what was the fitting bay.

Over the years, a number of changes have been made to the building, including the addition of an extra floor. The piles of tyres over the corner pillars have now been removed, as has the Bibendum. The tiles remain, however, highlighting the exuberance of the building and as a memory of the early days of the motor industry.

MICHELIN

MICHELIN

MICHELIN
HOUSE

BIBENDUM

COUPE GORDON-BENNETT
1904

THÉRY sur
RICHARD-BR

AN OVERHEAD CRANE AT NEW CROSS

The General Engine & Boiler Company occupy works in New Cross originally built for railway locomotive manufacture. In the days when locomotives were constructed there, the central section of the works consisted of three bays containing a foundry, a machine shop, and an assembly and fitting shop; over the middle bay still exists an overhead travelling crane believed to have been erected about 1853. This crane, designed on sound structural engineering principles, was originally used during assembly in the central area where there was sufficient space for two engines to be built simultaneously. Its stresses appear to have been calculated in an outstandingly competent manner, and indeed with only one exception, relating to running gear, no new design principles have been incorporated in this type of crane up to the present time.

The crane could certainly lift 10 tons, was probably safe to 15 tons and may have been used for loads up to 20 tons. Its length of travel was 60 ft with a span of 28 ft. The gantry is framed up inside the walls of the bay and consists of pitch-pine balks mainly of 12-inch-square sections. Railway lines are mounted on the balks for the longitudinal run. The crane beam is also of pitch-pine balks and closely resembles the modern construction used in overhead travelling cranes. The bogies at either end were built separately and the two main traverse beams are bolted to them and stiffened beneath by stay bars attached in the centre to cast-iron struts.

The 'long' travel was operated by a hand-crank at one end and the 'crab', which provides the traverse of the crane, was also hand-winched. There were three double-ended shafts on the 'crab' for the attachment of crank handles; one shaft operated the traverse, the other two the lifting mechanism which was based on a differential pulley block system. Even today this can be found in some overhead cranes.

The travelling crane remains in position exactly as it was when last used many years ago. It is now considered unsafe because the supporting gantry shows signs of rotting in several places. There is, however, no intention of dismantling this very fine specimen of the precursor of the modern lifting crane.

Another item of outstanding interest at the General Engine & Boiler Company works is a tensile testing machine shown in the second photograph. This machine was probably installed in 1873, and bears the legend 'Tangyes Engineers, Birmingham', the same Tangyes upon whom I. K. Brunel called in his last

desperate struggle to launch the *Great Eastern*.

The machine was, and still is, used to measure the tension that test-bars of various materials will withstand before breaking. The test-bar is clamped into jaws in the lower centre section of the unit; tension is applied to one jaw by means of a hydraulic jack pumped by the hand lever on the right of the photograph, the other jaw being connected to the weighing-machine bar at the top of the machine; pumping forces the weighing-machine beam to respond to the tension by moving against its light stop. The weight is slid along the top beam as the jack is pumped until tension reaches 1 ton. If further tension is required, the weights, which can also be seen in the photograph, are applied to the right-hand side and the sliding weight returned to the left-hand side of the machine for each ton weight added. The breaking limits can thus be measured.

The unit can test up to the equivalent of 100 tons per square inch which brings it well into the range of the high tensile metals of today, and is still used regularly to demonstrate to Admiralty inspectors that materials used for their contracts meet specifications.

THE COPPER MILL IN WALTHAMSTOW

The copper mill in Walthamstow stands on an ancient mill site on one of the streams flowing into the Lea valley. The earliest reference to the mill is in a conveyance dated 1659. In maps and documents it is variously referred to as a 'powder mill', an 'oyl mill' (for linseed) and a 'corn mill', illustrating its changing roles and vicissitudes.

In 1808 it was purchased by the British Copper Company and used for rolling ingots of copper into sheets, and for stamping copper objects, notably tokens,[38] such as that illustrated. During this period the copper was brought by sea from south Wales into the Thames and then up the Lea by barge.

In 1860 ownership of the mill passed to the East London Waterworks Company, which in 1854 had constructed an aqueduct from the site to their filter beds at Lea Bridge. They repaired the substantial brick buildings, then dilapidated, but cleared the site of everything else. Most of the brickwork in the surviving buildings is eighteenth century, but the base of the west wall of the weir shows evidence of being earlier, while the Waterworks Company appear to have completely rebuilt the east wall. A later structure was added to this wall, with a façade matching the other nineteenth-century one. One water wheel was adapted in 1861 for pumping and was used to drain the land acquired for the first reservoir (three reservoirs were completed north of the copper mill in 1863), and to raise water from a well. Later the tower was built within the original structure to house a 'Bull'-type engine which was also used for pumping water from a well.

The mill is now owned by the Metropolitan Water Board, and consists only of the large building with two hipped roofs carried on six long wooden beams of 9 in by 6 in cross-section. It is said that these are ships' timbers: they certainly show evidence of the ribs originally joined to them. The entire roof structure is supported by two cast-iron columns. At the base of the wall by the weir, the bricks clearly indicate the position of the water wheel. The sluice passes under the east side of the building. An ancient crane with a wooden jib used for unloading barges still remains on the site.[39]

GAS ENGINES AT LAMBETH

Engines using town gas were first developed by the Dowson Company, Westerham, Kent, in about 1876. Several other companies became active in this field, including Crossley, National, Andrews and Hornsby, but large engines were also imported from Belgium.

The engines in the smaller range were principally used for workshop drives and for farm power sources. The higher-powered engines were generally for industrial processes, some of the biggest being run on blast-furnace gas; their function was to generate electricity and to provide air blast for the furnaces. Those installed in the Stavely iron works in 1906 have only recently been superseded.

In the past the gas engine held a considerable advantage over steam in that it did not require a boiler and therefore occupied less space. Some of the early engines ran on producer gas which was cheap. However, they had the disadvantage of requiring highly skilled attendance and maintenance. They remained popular until about the 1920s when the wider electricity grid made electric power more economical.

The gas engines in the photograph were built by Hornsby in 1908 and 1911. They were rated at 49 bhp and 37 bhp respectively; both have an $11\frac{1}{2}$-in bore and 18-in stroke. The latter engine was supplied for driving printing machinery and had a heavier electric-lighting-type flywheel of about 3 tons, the smaller flywheel being $2\frac{1}{2}$ tons. These machines were virtually the end of the series since production ceased about 1912.

The two machines were adapted to their present use and location in the Hibberd Bros. factory in 1929, where they were synchronized and drove the joinery machinery in the plant. Today one engine is in daily use driving about three-quarters of all the machinery (the remainder is electrically powered). The other engine is kept for standby purposes. Town gas supplies are used, the gas passing through an anti-fluctuator to maintain a steady pressure. Oil pots are located on the cylinder and big end, and water for cooling is pumped from a natural well 30 ft underground.

GATE WINCH FROM THE ST KATHARINE DOCKS ENTRANCE

Two major problems associated with the handling and movement of goods by sea were the looting, pilfering and smuggling, and the difficulty of loading and unloading ships affected by the rise and fall of the tides. Both these problems were largely solved by the building of enclosed docks. On the landward side the enclosed dock made it difficult for thieves to enter or for smugglers to move their contraband; on the river side the dock enabled ships to lay alongside a quay unaffected by the state of the tide. This was achieved by the construction of massive hinged iron and wooden gates between dock and river.

The St Katharine Docks, which have perhaps suffered less change than most of the other major docks, are always associated with Thomas Telford, who was engineer of the project and supervised the work. It is the architect Philip Hardwick, however, to whom must be credited the elegance of the warehouses and the most pleasing design of the whole docks.

These consist of an Eastern and Western Dock, both entered from the Basin which is separated from the river by a lock. The original entrance to the Basin, constructed in 1820–28, consisted of side walls and a curved invert of lock built of stone blocks laid on fir planking over piles of beech and elm. The curved pointing cills were of timber, fastened to stone blocks, carried on a row of timber sheeting piles. The entrance was 290 ft long overall and the lock chamber 180 ft long and 45 ft wide. Originally there were three pairs of mitre gates each operated by hand-turned winches.

Joseph Bramah received a contract from the St Katharine Docks Company for sixteen gate winches; twelve of these were fixed at the entrance lock and the others in the cutting leading from the Basin to the Western Dock. A further four winches were provided for the Eastern Dock completed in 1829.

A major reconstruction of the Basin entrance took place in 1957 when the timber gates showed signs of decay above low-water level. Eight of the winches were still in position and an identical winch was found at the south-west corner of the Wapping Inner Lock, London Docks. In the course of reconstruction the hand winches were removed and replaced by electric ones. The winch illustrated was photographed on a scrap heap, and it has been deduced that it was of the batch supplied for the later contract for the Eastern Dock; it bears the date 1829. It was rescued by a Port of London official and is now preserved near the Basin. It worked with minimum maintenance and completely satisfactorily until its removal in 1957.

THE FIRST TELEVISION STUDIOS

In 1936 the BBC acquired part of Alexandra Palace, which dominates the heights of north London, to house its first television transmitter and studios. The Corporation's mast, now a familiar part of the London skyline, measures 220 ft, but added to the building height and ground rise reaches an overall height of 600 ft above sea level. The total building area rented was 55,000 sq. ft including an old theatre. The studios were 70 ft long, 30 ft wide and 23 ft high, and the lighting capacity between 50 and 70 kilowatts.

Two studios were equipped for transmission, each utilizing different methods. These were the Marconi-EMI system, and the mechanical or intermediate film system devised by John Logie Baird, the father of television, who had made successful demonstrations as early as 1926 in an attic at 21 Frith Street.

On 26 August 1936 special experimental transmissions were made to Radio-lympia. The first programme, introduced by Leslie Mitchell, was a variety show called 'Here's Looking at You'. A toss of a coin decided that the Baird system would transmit the programme, after which the two systems were used on alternate days.

The station, the first in the world to transmit regular high-definition programmes, was officially opened on 2 November 1936. The two systems were used in alternate weeks for about three months when the Television Advisory Committee reported against the mechanical system. From thereon the Marconi-EMI system, with its 405 lines, 50 pictures per second, interlaced scanning, was adopted permanently. This incorporated four Emitron cameras and a vision transmitter with a peak output of 17 kilowatts.

Regular transmissions continued until 1 September 1939 when, for security reasons, instructions to close the station were issued. It was not re-opened until 7 June 1946 and remained the only transmitting station for the London area until 1956 when it was replaced by the Crystal Palace. At the outset, studios and transmitter were located together, something unusual in the BBC. At the opening of the Lime Grove studios in 1950, studio and transmitter were again separated.

Only the BBC television news service now operates from Alexandra Palace, but innovation continues on the hills of north London. On 10 October 1955 the first experimental colour test transmissions took place from there. With the coming of regular colour television in 1967, there will be limited facilities for colour news items and it is possible that the studios will again take on an important role in a new stage of television development.

REMAINS OF THE PNEUMATIC DESPATCH RAILWAY

Twenty years after the last atmospheric train had run over the London, Brighton & South Coast rails, a new endeavour using the same principle commenced deep under the London streets in 1865. This was the Pneumatic Despatch Railway, built solely to carry letters and parcels from Euston station to the General Post Office in the City.

The first section, opened in 1865, consisted of a cast-iron-lined brick tunnel of roughly horseshoe shape, 4 ft 6 in wide and 4 ft high. Steam-driven suction fans sited at Holborn drew the air out of the tunnel by centrifugal force.

As the tunnel had to be kept reasonably airtight the cars were fitted with a rubber flange which clung tightly to the tube's interior lining. At stations, hermetically-sealed spring-loaded doors excluded the air. No driver was carried and speeds were controlled by an elaborate system of decelerating air conduits. An average speed of 35 mph was obtained and speeds approaching 60 mph were recorded on the down grade beneath Farringdon Street.

Nevertheless, like its predecessors, this atmospheric line was defeated by the inadequacies of the materials then available. The difficulty of keeping the tunnel airtight proved to be insuperable. After about eight or ten years (no one is certain, since operations became intermittent towards the end), the Pneumatic Despatch Railway ceased operations. The tunnel was forgotten.

Twenty years later George Threlfall, a consulting engineer, 'found' the tunnel again. A scheme was proposed to re-open the line, this time using electric power. The scheme apparently did not work, but precisely what happened to it and its sponsors is shrouded in mystery. Threlfall himself purchased the cast-iron tunnel linings and sold them, it is said, making a handsome profit. The railway passed into oblivion again for nearly forty years, until some road works in 1930 breached the tunnel; this time a number of mail cars were found, one of which is in the Bruce Castle Museum at Tottenham.

Most sections have now either been bricked up or filled in, but a length under Drummond Street is largely in its original condition. It is now a Post Office cable duct, but some of the rails still lie on the tunnel floor and along the sides the occasional ceramic insulator can be seen.

ACKNOWLEDGEMENTS

Most books are dependent upon more than just the skills of the author—it would be unusual for a book of this type not to have relied heavily upon the active assistance and co-operation of other people—far too many to name individually. They include many of London's librarians and borough and company archivists, trade-journal editors and those much-maligned professionals, the public-relations officers of large firms and organizations.

Very many individuals within companies have provided detailed information on buildings and equipment owned by their firms. Regrettably so much of interest which they have uncovered has had to be omitted for no better reason than lack of space. Their work is not wasted, however: everything located is to be passed to the Government's consultant on industrial monuments.

Special contributions were made by: William Campbell, the chief reference librarian of the Hornsey Central Library who, as with my other books, bore the brunt of my inquiries and requirements with patience and indeed fortitude; N. M. Bussell, on the Surrey Iron Railway; Peter W. Brooks, on London's early aerodromes; M. Bawtree, who willingly gave me access to his many years of research into coal and wine duty post locations. Identification of items was greatly assisted in East London by J. Downs; in Central London by H. G. Button; in West London by A. J. Errington; in North East London by W. G. S. Tonkins; in South West London by J. Ashdown; in Battersea by Miss Carol Hart and by G. Wyn Hamel. Tony Goulden's probing of a number of engineering items and C. E. C. Townsend's guidance on Port of London Authority equipment have been invaluable.

I am indebted to Christopher West for his investigations into the Bramah press, the Ram Brewery beam engines and the veneer lathe, and for his suggestions for many other lines of inquiry. The text was immeasurably improved by his careful reading and corrections and his expertise as a geographer.

The typing and ordering of the manuscript has been in the very capable hands of Mrs Marie Tucker.

I am grateful to Edwin Smith for the photograph of the façade of the Regents Park Diorama; to Hersey-Sparling Meter Company Ltd for the print of the water-meter testing tower at Belle Isle and to K. G. Jones for information on the tower; to the Western Region of British Rail for the early photograph of the Mint Stables; to Ferranti for the print of the Grosvenor Gallery generating station; to the

Illustrated London News for the prints of the Deptford Generating Station, of the Croydon Atmospheric Railway station and of the first attempt to launch the *Great Eastern*; and to A. C. Barrington Brown for the photograph of the Walthamstow copper-mill token.

It would be remiss of me not to acknowledge publicly the patience and care of Joseph McKeown, whose splendid and skilful photographs were produced despite my inadequate briefings. His feeling for his subject is so apparent as to require no comment from me except to thank him for the exceptionally high degree of co-operation and his many positive and practical suggestions for improving the book.

The organization and mechanics of the research were entirely the work of my research assistant, Penelope Vousden. The massive correspondence, indexing and recording system which she instituted never failed. Apart from conducting much of the basic field research, she was also responsible for many of the items included in the book and edited the whole manuscript. Her efficiency, tact and perseverance are the only reasons why both the author and photographer ever succeeded in completing this project.

Finally I must again thank my family and my colleagues for relieving me of domestic and professional duties which permitted me to devote the time necessary to the completion of this book.

It can be seen that this book more than most is the work of very many people, but the sins of omission and commission are entirely those of the author.

REFERENCES

1 Chaloner, W. H. and Musson, A. E. *A Visual History of Modern Britain—Industry & Technology.* Vista Books, 1963.

2 Went, D. 'The Five Tide Mills of Essex', *Essex Countryside* Aug/Sept 1960.

3 Ridding, A. *S. Z. de Ferranti—Pioneer of Electric Power.* HMSO, 1964.

4 A dramatic and moving account of the building of the Thames Tunnel is contained in L. T. C. Rolt's definitive biography *Isambard Kingdom Brunel.* Longmans, 1957.

5 Hall, P. G. *The Industries of London.* Hutchinson University Library, 1962.

6 *Victoria History of the Counties of England—Surrey.* Vol. 2. Constable, 1905.

7 Adburgham, A. *Shops and Shopping.* George Allen & Unwin, 1964.

8 Pevsner, N. *Buildings of England—London* (except the Cities of London and Westminster.) Vol. 1. Penguin Books, 1962.

9 Chadwick, E. *Report on the Sanitary Conditions of the Labouring Population.* 1842.

10 Pannell, J. P. M. *An Illustrated History of Civil Engineering.* Thames and Hudson, 1964.

11 Buchanan, R. A. *Technology and Social Progress.* Pergamon Press, 1965.

12 Barton, N. *The Lost Rivers of London.* Phoenix House, 1962.

13 Quoted by D. Chandler and A. D. Lacey in *The Rise of the Gas Industry in Britain.* British Gas Council, 1949.

14 O'Dea, W. *The Social History of Lighting.* Routledge & Kegan Paul, 1958.

15 White, H. P. *A Regional History of the Railways of Great Britain*, Vol 2, *Southern England.* David & Charles, 1961.

16 *The Victoria History of the Counties of England*, Vol 2, *Surrey.* Constable, 1905.

17 Fletcher, G. *London Overlooked.* Hutchinson, 1964.

18 Wills, G. 'The Kensington Potteries', *Apollo.* July 1956.

19 Chaloner, W. H. and Musson, A. E. *A Visual History of Modern Britain—Industry & Technology.* Vista Books, 1963.

20 Bawtree, M. *The London Coal Duties and Their Boundary Marks.* Paper read to the Rickmansworth Historical Society. 9 April 1964.

21 Richards, J. M. *The Functional Tradition.* Architectural Press, 1958.

22 *Progress—The Romance of a British Industry.* Otto Monsted Ltd, *circa* 1910.

23 *Ibid.*

24 Pritchett, V. S. *London Perceived.* Chatto & Windus, 1962.

25 Stacey, N. A. H. and Wilson, A. *The Changing Pattern of Distribution.* Pergamon Press, 1965.

26 *Tower Hamlets News.* 'The Silkweavers of Spitalfields and Bethnal Green'. Borough of Tower Hamlets. July 1965.

27 Spratt, H. P. *Outline History of Transatlantic Steam Navigation.* HMSO, 1950.

28 Armytage, W. H. G. *A Social History of Engineering.* Faber and Faber, 1961.

29 Rolt, L. T. C. *Isambard Kingdom Brunel.* Longmans, 1957.

30 Pevsner, N. *Buildings of England—London.* (except the Cities of London and Westminster.) Vol 1. Penguin Books, 1962. (Pevsner in fact quotes the wrong date, since the construction of the New Street stack of warehouses was commenced much earlier in 1770.)

31 Ceram, C. W. *Archaeology of the Cinema.* Thames & Hudson, 1965

32 Shepherd, T. H. and Elmes, J. *Metropolitan Improvements.* Jones & Co., 1829.

33 Hamilton Ellis, G. *London, Brighton and South Coast Railway.* Ian Allan, 1960.

34 Pannell, J. P. M. *An Illustrated History of Civil Engineering.* Thames and Hudson, 1964.

35 Hamilton Ellis, G. *London, Brighton and South Coast Railway.* Ian Allan, 1960.

36 Technical Information Sheet No. 13. London Transport, 1952.

37 Pannell, J. P. M. *An Illustrated History of Civil Engineering.* Thames and Hudson, 1964.

38 Mathias, P. *English Trade Tokens.* Abelard-Schuman, 1962.

39 Tonkins, W. G. S. 'The Coppermill—Walthamstow'. *The Record.* January 1966.

LOCATION INDEX

Locations of the items included in this book have been tabulated along with information on their accessibility. Most of the buildings can be seen easily from the public highway, for example the Abbey Mills pumping station; a few are completely accessible, as in the case of Smithfield Market. Most machinery included is neither visible nor accessible, but many of the organizations listed are prepared to permit inspection of the items on their premises if permission is sought. This, however, is a privilege, and it is hoped that in seeking permission the least possible inconvenience to owners of monuments is caused, so that others who may follow will not be refused.

Subject and Page No.		Location	Ownership	Inaccessible	Inaccessible but Visible	Accessible
Hydraulic devil	14	St Katharine Docks, East Smithfield, E1	Port of London Authority, Trinity Square, EC3	×	—	—
Tide mill	16	Three Mills Lane, Bromley-by-Bow, E3	Three Mills Bonded Warehouses Ltd, Three Mills Lane, Bromley-by-Bow, E3	—	×	—
Bramah press	18	Leatherhead Road, Chessington, Surrey	Ordnance Survey, Leatherhead Road, Chessington Surrey	×	—	—
Deptford East power station	20	Stowage Wharf, SE8	Central Electricity Generating Board, Bankside House, Sumner Street, SE1	—	×	—
Thames tunnel shaft	24	Behind Rotherhithe Station, SE16	London Transport, 55 Broadway, SW1	—	× (shaft)	× (tunnel)
Water wheel	28	Littlers Close, SW19	Merton Printers Ltd, Merton Abbey Printworks, Littlers Close, SW19	—	×	—
Piano factory	30	12 Oval Road, NW1	Property Holding & Investment Trust Ltd, Empire House St Martin's le Grand, EC1	—	×	—

Subject and Page No.		Location	Ownership	Inaccessible	Inaccessible but Visible	Accessible
Capital Patent Crane	32	20 St Swithin's Lane, EC4	Geo. G. Sandeman Sons & Co. Ltd, 20 St Swithin's Lane, EC4	×	—	—
Abbey Mills pumping station	34	Abbey Lane, E15	Greater London Council, 10 Great George Street, SW1	—	×	—
Gasholder	38	Fulham Gasworks, SW6	North Thames Gas Board, Monck Street, SW1	×	—	—
Veneer lathe	40	Avon Wharf, E3	John Wright & Sons (Veneers) Ltd, Avon Wharf, E3	—	×	—
Control tower	42	Purley Way, Croydon	Terminal Buildings (Holdings) Ltd, High House, East Ayton, Scarborough	—	×	—
Sewer-gas lamp	44	Carting Lane, Strand, WC2	Maintained by: North Thames Gas Board, Monck Street, SW1	—	---	×
Track of Croydon, Merstham & Godstone railway	46	Purley Rotary Field, Purley	London Borough of Croydon Town Hall, Croydon	—	—	×
		or: just south of Joliffe Arms on A 23, south of Hooley	British Rail, Southern Region, Victoria Station, SW1	—	—	×
Hand-printing press	48	133 Fonthill Road, Finsbury Park, N4	Hunnings Printing Works, 133 Fonthill Road, Finsbury Park, N4	×	—	—
Umbrella shop	50	James Smith (Umbrellas) Ltd, 32 New Oxford Street, WC1	Crown Estate Office, Whitehall, SW1	—	—	×
Pottery kiln	52	Walmer Road, W11	White & Co. Ltd, 120 London Road, North End Junction, Portsmouth	—	×	—
Planing machine	54	Footscray Road, Eltham, SE9	Walter Grafton & Son, Ltd, Footscray Road, Eltham, SE9	×	—	—

Subject and Page No.	Location	Ownership	Inaccessible	Inaccessible but Visible	Accessible
Candle factory 56	Belmont Works, SW11	Price's Patent Candle Co. Ltd, Belmont Works, SW11	×	—	—
Coal duty posts 58	Rickmansworth Road, Near Prince of Wales	Corporation of the City of London, Guildhall, EC3	—	—	×
Water-meter testing tower 60	Tileyard Road, York Way, N7	Ebonite Container Co. (Manufacturing) Ltd, Tileyard Road York Way, N7	—	×	—
Container hoist 64	Central Street, City Road, EC1	British Road Services, Melbury House, Melbury Terrace, NW1	×	—	—
Cold rolling machine 66	Hancock Road, Bromley-by-Bow, E3	Ratner Safe Co. Ltd, Hancock Road, Bromley-by-Bow, E3	×	—	—
Round House engine shed 68	Chalk Farm Road, NW1	Centre 42 20 Fitzroy Square, W1	—	×	—
Food-drying kilns 70	South Lambeth Road, Vauxhall, SW8	Brand & Co. Ltd, South Lambeth Road, Vauxhall, SW8	—	×	—
Hermitage Inner Cutting swing bridge 72	London Dock, East Smithfield, E1	Port of London Authority, Trinity Square, EC3	×	—	—
Margarine factory 74	Bridge Road, Southall, Middlesex	Unilever Ltd, Unilever House, EC4	—	×	—
Ether plant 78	Howards of Ilford Ltd, Uphall Road, Ilford	Laporte Industries Ltd, 14 Hanover Square W1	×	—	—
Lifting machinery 80	Tower Bridge, SE1	Bridge House Estates Committee, Corporation of London, EC2	×	—	—
Roof of Smithfield Market 82	Smithfield Market, EC1	Central Markets Committee, Corporation of the City of London, EC2	—	—	×

Subject and Page No.	Location	Ownership	Inaccessible	Inaccessible but Visible	Accessible
Silk Weavers' houses 84	Fournier Street, E1	Various	—	×	—
Fairground music punch 88	31 Eyre Street Hill, EC1	Chiappa Ltd, 31 Eyre Street Hill, EC1	×	—	—
Mint Stables 90	Winsland Street, W2	British Rail, Western Region, Paddington, W2	—	×	—
Great Eastern launching site 92	Napier Yard, Millwall, E14	Joseph Westwood & Co. Ltd, Napier Yard, Millwall, E14	—	×	—
Roof of Porter Tun Room 96	Chiswell Street, EC1	Whitbread & Co. Ltd, Chiswell Street, EC1	×	—	—
Sealing-wax factory 98	Verney Road, SE16	Cooper, Dennison & Walkden Ltd, Walkden Works, Verney Road, SE16	×	—	—
Plate edge-planer 100	Ferry Street, Millwall, E14	John Fraser & Son Ltd, Ferry Street, Millwall, E14	×	—	—
Wooden winch 102	St Paul's Cathedral EC4		—	—	×
Bell lathe 104	32 Whitechapel Road, E1	Whitechapel Bell Foundry, 32 Whitechapel Road, E1	×	—	—
Cornish engine 106	Pumping Station, Kew Bridge, Surrey	Metropolitan Water Board, New River Head, Rosebery Avenue, EC1	—	×	—
Snuff mills 108	Morden Hall Park, Morden	The National Trust, 42 Queen Anne's Gate, SW1	—	×	—
East India Company warehouse 110	Cutler Street E1	Port of London Authority, Trinity Square, EC3	—	×	—
Clock gearwheel-cutting machine 112	15 Bowling Green Lane, EC1	Thwaites & Reed Ltd, 15 Bowling Green Lane, EC1	×	—	—
Regents Park Diorama 114	9-10 Park Square East, NW1	Bedford College, Regents Park, NW1	—	×	—

Subject and Page No.		Location	Ownership	Inaccessible	Inaccessible but Visible	Accessible
Pumping house— atmospheric railway	116	Water Works Yard, Surrey Street, Croydon	Croydon Water Department, 43 Wellesley Road, Croydon	—	×	—
Linoleum press	120	Staines, Middlesex	Linoleum Manufacturing Co. Ltd, Staines, Middlesex	×	—	—
Tram tunnel	122	Junction of Theobalds Road & Southampton Row, WC1	London Transport, 55 Broadway, SW1	—	×	—
Windmill	126	Blenheim Gardens, SW2	Greater London Council, County Hall, SE1	—	×	—
Wharncliffe Viaduct	128	Hanwell, Middlesex	British Rail, Western Region, Paddington, W2	—	×	—
Beam engine	130	The Ram Brewery, Wandsworth, SW18	Young & Co.'s Brewery Ltd, Wandsworth SW18	×	—	—
Catacombs	132	Camden Goods Station, Oval Road, NW1	British Rail, London Midland Region, St Pancras Chambers, Euston Road, NW1	×	—	—
Michelin tyre works	134	Michelin House, 81 Fulham Road, SW3	Michelin Tyre Co. Ltd, Michelin House, 81 Fulham Road, SW3	—	×	—
Overhead crane	136	Hatcham Iron Works Pomeroy Street, Works, New Cross, SE14	The General Engine & Boiler Co. Ltd, Pomeroy Street, New Cross, SE14	×	—	—
Copper mill	140	Coppermill Lane, E17	Metropolitan Water Board, New River Head, Rosebery Avenue, EC1	—	×	—
Hornsby gas engines	142	Dorset Works, 66 Meadow Road, South Lambeth, SW8	Hibberd Bros. Ltd, Dorset Works, 66 Meadow Road, South Lambeth, SW8	×	—	—

Subject and Page No.		Location	Ownership	Inaccessible	Inaccessible but Visible	Accessible
Gate winch	144	St Katharine Docks, East Smithfield, E1	Port of London Authority, Trinity Square, EC3	×	—	—
TV studios	146	Alexandra Palace, N22	BBC, Broadcasting House, W1	×	—	—
Pneumatic Despatch Railway	148	Corner of Drummond Street & Hampstead Road, NW1	Post Office, Headquarters Building, St Martins-le-Grand, EC1	×	—	—

INDEX

Aeolian Hall, 11, 20
Aesthetic Movement, the, 28
Aiken, Henry, 52
Alexandra Palace, 146
All Hallows-by-the-Tower Church, 112
Armstrong, 10

Bacon, Francis, 9
Baird, John Logie, 10, 146
Barker, Robert, 10, 114
Barry, John Wolfe, 80
Bazalgette, Joseph, 10, 34
Big Ben, 80
Binns, Thomas, 56
Booth, Charles, 52
Boulton, 10
Boulton & Watt, 96, 106
Bramah, Joseph, 10, 18, 144
Brunel, Isambard Kingdom, 10, 24, 80, 92, 94, 116, 138
Brunel, Marc, 10, 24, 26
Butterley Iron Works, 46

Campbell-Black, Tom, 42
Carlton House, 38
Caxton, William, 48
Chadwick, 10, 34
Clementi, Muzio, 30
Chiappi, 88
Crystal Palace, 146
Clouston, A. E., 42
Coal Exchange, 10
Collard & Collard, 30
Cubitt, William, 116

Dance, Thomas, 70
Dickens, Charles, 52
Dowson Company, 142

Edison, Thomas, 20
Eros, 80
Espinasse, M., 134
Evelyn, John, 20

Fairburn, William, 16
Faraday, Michael, 78
Farmer & Rogers, 28
Ferrand, Clermont, 134
Ferranti, Sebastian de, 10, 20, 22
Fielding & Platt, 120
Fortnum & Mason, 112
Fox, James, 54
Froude, William, 92
Fulham Gasholder, 38

Grafton, Walter, & Sons Ltd., 54
Grand Junction Water Works Company, 106
Grant, John, 36
Gray, J. M., 92

Great Eastern, the, 92, 95, 138
Greaves, Brook, 102
Grosvenor Gallery, 11, 20
Guildhall Library, 112
Gutenberg, Johann, 48

Halfhide, William, 28
Hanson, A. B., 74
Hardwick, Philip, 144
Hazelwood House, 50
Hewes, T. C., 16
Hibberd Brothers, 142
Holland, Henry, 110
Hudson, Kenneth, 6, 10, 38
Hummiston, Willis, 56
Hydraulic quay cranes, 14

Jessop, William, 46
Johnson, Amy, 42
Joliffe Arms Hotel, 46
Jones, Horace, 80, 82
Jupp, Richard, 110

King's Head Brewery, 96
Kirby-Green, Betty, 42
Koch, Robert, 34
Kremlin, the, 36

Leinster Terrace, 13
Liberty, Arthur, 10, 28
Lindberg, Charles, 42
Lister, Robert, 78
Littler, Edmund, 28
Lombe, John, 84
London & Croydon Railway Co., 116
London Electricity Supply Corporation, 20, 22
London Hydraulic Mains Company, 12
London Underground, 26
Long, Dr Crawford, 78

Maudslay, Henry, 106
Mège-Mouriez, 74
Metropolitan Board of Works, 34
Metropolitan Railway, 13
Mitchell, Armstrong, 80
Mitchell, Leslie, 146
Mollison, Jim, 42
Monsted, Otto, 10, 74, 76
Morgan, James, 114
Morgan, Joseph, 56
Morris, Herbert, 64
Morris, William, 28
Murdoch, 10, 38
Murray, Matthew, 54

Nash, John, 114
Newcomen, Thomas, 16
Nightingale, Florence, 34

Palmer, William, 56
Pasteur, Louis, 34
Peter the Great, 20
Pevsner, 30
Piper, David, 13
Porter Tun Room, 96
Pugin, J. G., 114

Ratner Safe Company, 66
Rennie, John, 10, 72, 96
Roberts, Richard, 54
Royal Dockyard, 20
Russell, John Scott, 10, 92, 94

Sandeman, George, 32
Savery, Thomas, 16
Savoy Hotel, 44
Scott, Charles, 42
Scott, Walter, 38
Simmons, Prof Jack, 7
Smeaton, John, 10, 16, 96
Smith, Beacock & Tannet, 100
Smith, James, & Sons, 50
Snow, Dr John, 34
Stainthorp, John, 56
Stephenson, 10, 38
St Katharine Docks, 144
Surrey Iron Railway Company, 46

Tangye Brothers, 94, 138
Telford, Thomas, 10, 144
Three Mills, 16
Threlfall, George, 148
Thwaites & Reed, 112
Tower Bridge, 10, 80
Tower of London, 18
Trevithick, 10, 24
Tuck, Joseph, 56
Tylor's, 60

Vivian, Andrew, 106

Walkden, Richard, 98
Walker, James, 102
Walker, Tannet, 14
Wallington Public Library, 46
Walton, Frederick, 120
Waterlow, 10
Watt, James, 10, 16, 96
Webb, J. E., 44
Wentworth & Sons, 130
Westminster Hall, 96
Wharncliffe, Lord, 10
Whitbread Brewery, 96
Whitbread, Samuel, 10
Whitworth, Joseph, 10, 54
Winsor, 10, 38
Wright, John, 40

Young's Ram Brewery, 130